THE WHATEVER FACTOR

A Salvation Theory for Thinkers

TERRY POOLER

Copyright © 2016 by Terry Pooler

The Whatever Factor
A Salvation Theory for Thinkers
by Terry Pooler

Printed in the United States of America.

ISBN 9781498480932

All rights reserved solely by the author. The author guarantees all contents are original and do not infringe upon the legal rights of any other person or work. No part of this book may be reproduced in any form without the permission of the author. The views expressed in this book are not necessarily those of the publisher.

Unless otherwise indicated, Scripture quotations taken from the Holy Bible, New International Version (NIV). Copyright © 1973, 1978, 1984, 2011 by Biblica, Inc.™. Used by permission. All rights reserved.

Scripture quotations taken from the American Standard Version (ASV)) – *public domain.*

Scripture quotations taken from the English Standard Version (ESV). Copyright © 2001 by Crossway, a publishing ministry of Good News Publishers. Used by permission. All rights reserved.

Scripture quotations taken from the King James Version (KJV) – *public domain.*

Scripture quotations taken from The Message (MSG). Copyright © 1993, 1994, 1995, 1996, 2000, 2001, 2002. Used by permission of NavPress Publishing Group. Used by permission. All rights reserved.

Scripture quotations taken from the New American Standard Bible (NASB). Copyright © 1960, 1962, 1963, 1968, 1971, 1972, 1973, 1975, 1977, 1995 by The Lockman Foundation. Used by permission. All rights reserved.

Scripture quotations taken from the New Century Version (NCV). Copyright © 2005 by Thomas Nelson, Inc. Used by permission. All rights reserved.

Scripture quotations taken from the New King James Version (NKJV). Copyright © 1982 by Thomas Nelson, Inc. Used by permission. All rights reserved.

Scripture quotations taken from the Holy Bible, New Living Translation (NLT). Copyright ©1996, 2004, 2007 by Tyndale House Foundation. Used by permission of Tyndale House Publishers, Inc.

Scripture quotations taken from the New Revised Standard Version (NRSV). Copyright © 1989 the Division of Christian Education of the National Council of the Churches of Christ in the United States of America.

Scripture quotations taken from the Revised Standard Version (RSV). Copyright © 1946, 1952, and 1971 the Division of Christian Education of the National Council of the Churches of Christ in the United States of America. Used by permission. All rights reserved.

Scripture quotations taken from the The Holy Bible, Modern English Version. Copyright © 2014 by Military Bible Association. Published and distributed by Charisma House. All rights reserved.

www.xulonpress.com

Acknowledgments

To Mark Goldstein who said, "Pastor you *must* write a book about your *Whatever Factor* concept. You answer questions that no one else in the Christian literary world has done. You *must!*" Mark knows how to get into my head and force me to think bigger and believe impossible things can really come to fruition.

To my editor, Michelle Nash, who said after editing my manuscript, "Terry, this is GREAT stuff. It has changed my life. You *must* publish it." With a heart for ministry and the gifts of an astute English teacher, she is an eternal optimist who never gives up.

To my wife Helene who, when weekend after weekend saw me hunched over my computer rather than relaxing with her, said… nothing! She has the intuitive patience and devoted love as my best friend and companion to know that allowing me to quietly work was her most loving support.

Disclaimer:

Who Should *Not* Read This Book

Not all Christian readers will benefit by reading this book. Do not continue reading if one or more of these defines you:
- You get easily upset when a cherished belief is questioned.
- You are easily discouraged by a suggestion that your current theology is inadequate.
- You are at a stage in life where your belief system must be very structured. (Note: This is not meant as a put-down statement, but merely an observation from long experience in ministry.)

Here are a couple examples for the third qualifier:

Some senior citizens have lost so much of what once offered a sense of stability and security etc, their health, death of close friends and family members, dwindling finances and lifestyle opportunities. As such, the one thing that *must* remain stable and secure is their theology, their one remaining constant. Hearing their cherished beliefs affirmed offers comfort.

On the other hand, some younger adults have been ravaged by a devastating self-chosen lifestyle or been victimized by abuse and pain. Their bodies, minds, and emotions are so wounded that they have no clue how to live a responsible, disciplined life. Like infants, unable yet to trust their own abilities to consistently choose what is good and proper and healthy, they need a structured and comfortable belief system (the "faith of their **father**," if you will) to hold them responsible during times of healing and transition.

Who *Should* Read This Book?

So, for whom is this book written?
- If your belief system requires you to become "worthy enough" to enter heaven by your ever-intensifying efforts to live a holy and spiritually disciplined life.
- If you are never sure that spiritually you have done *enough*.
- If you've been told that, once you've accepted Christ that your "salvation is secure," but you sometimes feel a nagging doubt.
- If you're troubled with the idea that God will take people to heaven against their will because they had a sincere conversation yet later renounced their belief in God.
- If you've experienced a tragic faith-destroying experience.
- If you're simply tired of religion and want no part of it.
- If you cannot harmonize your understanding of Scripture and common sense with the "security of salvation" theory.

Then this book is a *must* for you!

There remain many—in all age or culture or denominational brackets—who are up for the adventure of exploring the very words of Jesus Himself:

Disclaimer:

So I say to you: Ask and it will be given to you; seek and you will find; knock and the door will be opened to you. Luke 11:9 (NIV)

Jesus tells His followers to "search with all your heart." And the implication is that this search never ends AND the rewards will be increasingly gratifying.

If you believe that "nothing can separate you from the love of Christ," then my prayer is that the windows of your soul will open wider and the fresh breeze of God's loving and freeing Spirit will bring life to your spiritual walk.

Embrace the challenge—with just one caveat: Once you start, resolve to finish. The section, "The Whatever Factor Difference" *could* change your life. Now. And forever.

Let the Ask-Seek-Find journey begin!

Table of Contents

Section I – First Things

Disclaimer: Who should and shouldn't read this book.... vii
Introduction: Bar Code Salvation 15

Section II – Remedying the Security of Salvation Dysfunction
Chapter 1: The "Whatever" Factor 25
Chapter 2: Sincerely Uncertain About Assurance........ 39
Chapter 3: Isn't Sincerity at the Altar Enough 53
Chapter 4: Why Conversion Isn't Enough 75
Chapter 5: Salvation Is Not a Birthright............... 87
Chapter 6: Would You Marry a Nymphomaniac 101

Section III – Rethinking Heavenly Rewards
Chapter 7: The Dark Side of Heaven 117
Chapter 8: Living Under an Old or New Testament
           Concept of Heavenly Rewards 125
Chapter 9: The Reward of Common Experience 145

Section IV – Reaping The Whatever Factor Difference
Chapter 10: Heaven Is for Disciples.................. 163
Chapter 11: Heaven Is for Lovers.................... 177
Chapter 12: How Far Is Heaven 190
Chapter 13: The Whatever Factor Reaches
            into Your Wallet 204

Section V – Realizing that Whatever Is Forever
Chapter 14: Heaven Is for People Whom Jesus Would
            Enjoy Forever 217

Section I:

Introduction

Introduction: Bar Code Salvation

*"I like your Christ, I do not like your Christians.
You Christians are so unlike your Christ."*
Mahatma Gandhi

If you're not a Christian, then you'll probably nod in agreement with Gandhi. And if you are a Christian, it probably will raise your eyebrow.

Usually when I'm in a crowd of people whom I don't know, I keep my Christian profession a secret until an appropriate time. Why? Because often what they associate with the term "Christian" is not positive. In conversation with strangers, I'd rather develop a rapport without labels or preconceptions.

I remember sitting at a Bed & Breakfast table with eight other patrons and immediately feeling an inner resistance toward one couple. Without their saying such, I sensed—by their self-confident, arrogant behavior—that they were a certain type of Christian. The message I received was: "We're born again Christians. We have the only right answers, AND we've love to set you straight."

Later I realized one other thing: I didn't trust them. That's unfortunate to hear from a life-time Christian and pastor of forty-three years. Even though there are a LOT of admirably genuine Christians, I've discovered that too often the more "godly" a person looks and talks, the more likely he or she is to be using Christianity as a cover for unresolved, destructive personal issues. Sad, but true.

And, no, I'm not saying that I'm the perfect model of a Christ follower. In fact, I've had my moments. Here's one of my more benign examples. One day I was rushing to church with my mind frantically reviewing my morning sermon and worrying about the flow of the worship service.

I sped away from a stop light (exceeding the speed limit by a "safe" margin) and immediately overtook an extremely slow driver in the fast lane. Because of cars to my right who were going the same pokey speed (way below the speed limit) blocking me in, I was stuck. Putt, putt, putt! SO many un-Christian thoughts flashed through my mind, e.g, tailgating, honking, or even a less-than-friendly hand gesture. I was on a "mission for God" and they were getting in my way!

Finally, I navigated into the left turn lane at a stop light, relieved that I could finally shake them. Then it happened. That pokey driver turned into the same lane just ahead of me. No! It can't be! But it was TRUE. I followed him down the side street and... you guessed it... he pulled into my church parking lot. Can you imagine how effective my sermon would have been had I acted out my ungodly thoughts? I was SO relieved that I had not expressed my frustration and ruined an opportunity for God to touch a life.

All Christians fall short of the glory of God. We're each a work in progress. But my greatest concern is that some Christian teachings have the potential of actually encouraging and excusing ungodly behavior.

Thus, I return to my opening quote by Gandhi, which has its roots nearly a hundred years ago: *I like your Christ. I do not like your Christians...*

Introduction: Bar Code Salvation

Reverend W. P. King' (then pastor of the First Methodist Church of Gainesville, Georgia) in 1926 reviewed[1] the famed preacher Dr. E. Stanley Jones's sermon *The Christ of the Indian Road*.[2] His review includes the following:

> Dr. Jones says that the greatest hindrance to the Christian gospel in India is a dislike for western domination, western snobbery, the western theological system, western militarism and western race prejudice. Gandhi, the great prophet of India, said, "I love your Christ, but I dislike your Christianity." The embarrassing fact is that India judges us by our own professed standard.
>
> In reply to a question of Dr. Jones as to how it would be possible to bring India to Christ, Gandhi replied: "First, I would suggest that all of you Christians live more like Jesus Christ. Second, I would suggest that you practice your Christianity without adulterating it. The anomalous situation is that most of us would be equally shocked to see Christianity doubted or put into practice. Third, I would suggest that you put more emphasis on love, for love is the soul and center of Christianity..."

Did Gandhi really say that? There is some thought to the contrary, perhaps because we Christians don't like what he said. And maybe it hurts to hear the truth about ourselves — me included.

---

[1] *The Atlanta Constitution*, 7 February 1926, p. F14.

[2] Published in 1925 by The Abington Press, New York City.

But Gandhi is not alone. In his compelling book *Revolution* (2012), George Barna laments the considerable "disconnection between what research consistently shows about [the conduct of] churched Christians and what the Bible calls us to [actually] be... If Christians are what they claim to be," adds Barna, "their lives should be noticeably and compellingly different from the norm."[3]

David Kinnaman has researched this phenomenon for decades. In *unChristian* (2012), he writes about the palpable "lifestyle gap" between what Christians profess to believe and how they actually live. Kinnaman argues that Christianity in America has a well-deserved hypocritical image. "Our lives don't match our beliefs. In many ways, our lifestyles and perspectives are no different from those of anyone around us.[4]

Based on 2007 data, Kinnaman continues:

> "[W]e found that most of the lifestyle activities of born-again Christians were statistically equivalent to those of [non-Christians]. When asked to identify their activities over the last thirty days, born-again believers were just as likely to bet or gamble, to visit a pornographic Web site, to take something that did not belong to them, to consult a medium or psychic, to physically fight or abuse someone, to have consumed enough alcohol to be considered legally drunk, to have used an illegal, nonprescription drug, to have said something to someone that was not true....
>
> In the area of inappropriate sexual behavior—including looking at online pornography, viewing sexually explicit magazines or movies,

---

[3] George Barna, *Revolution*, p. 31.

[4] David Kinnaman, *unChristian*, p. 46

Introduction: Bar Code Salvation

or having a sexual encounter outside of marriage—30 percent of born-again Christians admitted to at least one of these activities in the past thirty days, compared to 35 percent of other [non-Christian] Americans. **In statistical and practical terms, this means the two groups are essentially no different from each other.**[5]

As a Christian one must ask, "How can this be?" One answer might lie in the following quiz:
1. Can I earn salvation by trying hard to obey God's will?
2. Am I saved because the penalty for sin is death and Jesus died my death for me?
3. Am I saved because Jesus obeyed God's perfect will and gives me forgiveness for my failure to obey His will?
4. Am I saved because God still requires perfect obedience to His will, but Jesus offers me His perfect obedience in place of my imperfect obedience?
5. Am I saved simply because I accept Jesus' forgiveness and perfect obedience on my behalf even if I subsequently have little or no interest in obeying God's will in my daily life?

If you are a Christian, questions 1-4 were probably pretty easy. But what about question 5? Is it really possible to be saved if we have little or no interest in changing our lifestyle to align with God's will? Most Evangelicals[6] would, almost

---

[5] Kinnaman, p. 47

[6] The National Association of Evangelicals defines "Evangelical" as: "A vibrant and diverse group, including believers found in many churches, denominations and nations." Not all Evangelicals believe the same but most in the Baptist, Pentecostal and Holiness groups do believe in the "security-of-salvation" doctrine. Thus, I use the term "Evangelical" in this book in a rather inclusive manner designating those, irrespective of denomination, who hold to this unique teaching.

grudgingly, reply "yes." Dr. Charles Stanley in his book *Eternal Security* (2002) answers: "Even if a believer for all practical purposes becomes an unbeliever, his salvation is not in jeopardy" (93).

Perhaps you believe you cannot be saved by human effort, for salvation is a gift of God. But will you be saved if you have a "WHATever, I'm-only-human" attitude toward obeying Him? The traditional Protestant position is that salvation is offered solely because of God's grace and can never be earned by holy deeds. Does that mean that being saved is never jeopardized?

A popular Christian bumper sticker reads: "Christians aren't perfect, just forgiven." Does this suggest that salvation works like a bar code? If, at some time, you "accepted Jesus," God was affected in the same way a bar code affects the check-out scanner. You can continue to be mean, selfish or lustful, but because you "accepted Jesus" you are given a pass through the heavenly gates.

The thought is that an appropriate amount of righteousness is shifted from Christ's account to your account in the bank of heaven and all your debts are paid. You are, accordingly, "saved." Your guilt is erased. Your sin debt account serviced — for past, present AND future.

In other words, you CANNOT be lost.

What a fail-safe, potentially low-commitment system. Yes, we SHOULD want our characters to be transformed to reflect Jesus' love. But in the end, does it affect our salvation, as long as we have our "conversion ticket" punched?[7]

Perhaps the reason many don't choose Christianity is because in their souls they know that there's just something wrong with this theory AND/OR they have been so turned off

---

[7] The Evangelical says that our behavior DOES matter, but not as far as our salvation is concerned. It only matters when it comes to what rewards one will receive AFTER they get to heaven. We'll talk about this in the chapter: "Holy Living Earns Heavenly Rewards."

Introduction: Bar Code Salvation

by "saved" Christians who lie, steal, and gossip while boasting about being "right" and "saved."

Recently the Jesus-embracing rock star Bono commented, "Christians are hard to tolerate. I don't know how Jesus does it."

In this Bar Code Theory, the essential thing is a person's "accepting Jesus moment." The life we live today or tomorrow has no necessary connection to our salvation, as long as the bar code does its job. Yes, we hear a lot of sermons stressing what a "good" Christian should or should not do: "We're not saved by works but by grace alone. And BECAUSE we are saved we OUGHT to at least try to obey God's will."

But the little voice in one's mind whispers: "So, it is not necessary to be good in order to *remain* saved?"

The apostle Peter once said: *"Believe on the Lord Jesus Christ and thou shalt be saved."* Acts 16:31 (KJV) Does this mean that because you once said, "I accept Jesus Christ as my Lord and Savior," you are then guaranteed heaven even if you thereafter choose to live a decadent, immoral, dishonest, and self-centered life?

To put it another way, is God obliged to save you just because at some point you accepted His grace, even though your behavior and character in no way reflects the teachings and life of Jesus'?

Thinking people ask, "Is there another option, one that makes more sense, respects our free will, transforms our character, and is wholly based on God's grace? There MUST be. And I believe there is.

After forty-three years of pastoring, traveling abroad for presentations, and writing, my experience tells me that maybe there's a better option: one that makes more sense and doesn't violate logic, respects our free will, transforms our character, and is wholly based on God's grace. I believe the Bible teaches a concept that gives clarity and hope both to the "security-of-salvation" believers and the "work-hard-to-be-worthy-of-heaven" Christians. I call it the "What*ever* Factor." It's 100%

biblical—and 100% transforming. It could even cause Gandhi to rethink his statement about liking the Christian's God, but not the Christian.

This is what I wish to explore with you during the next few chapters as together we "rethink" salvation-security.

Section II:

Remedying the Security of Salvation Dysfunction

Chapter 1:

The "Whatever" Factor

Mark's gaze was intense, his voice firm. "Pastor, you *have* to write a book about your 'Whatever' concept. You answer key questions that no one else in the Christian literary world has done. You *must*."

His credibility was notable. As president of the Central Florida Christian Chamber of Commerce, he interacted with a diversity of Christian leaders and pastors including Clark Whitten, author of *Pure Grace*.[8] Thankfully Mark persisted, and "The Whatever Factor" book is my attempt to answer *that* question for you.

Whitten's book, along with Charles Stanley's *Eternal Security*[9] (and similar books) enjoy wide acclaim among conservative Christians. But they fail to resolve the serious flaws in their "security-of-salvation" discussion that too often can result in arrogant, selfish, and judgmental Christians. Flaws that elicit questions like:

---

[8] Destiny Image Publishers, Shippensburg, 2012.

[9] Thomas Nelson Publishing, Nashville, 1990.

- Is one's security wholly based on a nebulous feeling of "just knowing" you were sincere at your conversion, as these authors claim?
- If a person accepts Jesus, but later denies his faith, will God take him to heaven against his will or *manipulate* him into returning to faith before he dies?
- Is heaven for those who merely have a "come to Jesus" moment with no subsequent character change or for those who worked hard to *earn* it?
- Is God a bookkeeper—or a lover?

The Whatever Factor: What Ever *Is* It?

Words often take on varied meanings depending on the inflection of the voice. While ministering for a few days in Tasmania (that lovely island south of mainland Australia), a man in his Aussie brogue remarked, "You Americans use the word 'interesting' in so many different ways. You use it to express sincere interest or to express doubt or even to deflect giving an honest answer. It depends on how you say it."

I found that observation *interesting!*

"Whatever" is another word whose meaning varies depending on inflection. Understanding these differences is vital to this discussion. Here are my two definitions as they relate to religion and spirituality:

WHAT'-ever (with accent on "WHAT" and the dropping of the voice with "ever"): An attitude that expresses indifference or even annoyance, e.g, "That's what you believe and that's fine if it works for you, but I don't see it that way so don't get all evangelistic by trying to convert me to your conviction. And definitely don't get judgmental by putting me down for believing differently." Accompanying gestures might include a slight tipping of the head back with an eye roll complimented by the shrugging of the shoulders and splaying out the hands, palms up.

The "Whatever" Factor

What -EVER' (Start with a low tone on "What," then raise the voice and accent "EVER."): An attitude that expresses a strong commitment. An expression of inclusiveness. A manner of expressing my worshipful attitude toward serving God.
Examples (all from NKJV):
1. "Whether you eat or drink, or whatEVER you do, do all to the glory of God." I Corinthians 10:31 [Emphasis mine here and in the following]
2. "Finally, brethren, whatEVER things are true, whatEVER things are noble, whatEVER things are just, whatEVER things are pure, whatEVER things are lovely, whatEVER things are of good report, if there is any virtue and if there is anything praiseworthy—meditate on these things." Philippians 4:8
3. And Jesus' words: "You are My friends if you do whatEVER I command you." John 15:4

For centuries that last one-liner by Jesus has troubled many Christians in light of the following: "Be ye therefore perfect, even as your Father which is in heaven is perfect," Matthew 5:48 (*KJV*), eliciting questions such as:
- How *does* one become perfect or holy enough to be assured of salvation?
- Who is the most righteous person that has lived in your lifetime or even in the last one hundred years? Mother Theresa, who devoted her life to loving and bringing Jesus' compassion to the outcasts of India? Billy Graham (a rare religious personality not plagued by scandal), who has devoted a lifetime to inviting the masses to make a "decision" to accept Jesus Christ?
- Where would you rank your pastor in regards to living a perfectly righteous life?
- Where in this hierarchy of righteous people would you place yourself? Do you feel even close to being "righteous"?

The solemn truth is that none of these so-called righteous people have considered themselves to be perfect. (If your pastor believes that he/she is the exception, do some church searching... fast!)

In fact, nobody—other than Jesus Christ—has lived a perfect life on this earth. *Not one!* Yet, some zealous Christians continue to teach that one MUST be perfect to be saved.

But in our heart's honest moments we KNOW we cannot achieve what Mother Theresa, Billy Graham, or even your pastor has. So, *what must I DO to have God's saving grace applied to my imperfection?* Intuitively, it feels like something we must DO.

In the Matthew 19 familiar story, the rich young ruler asked Jesus, "What must I DO to inherit eternal life?" Jesus told him to keep the commandments, to which he responded, "I have since my youth, but what do I lack?"

This lacking gnaws in all our souls. Scripture states, "Believe in the Lord Jesus Christ and you shall be saved." Yet in Matthew 7 Jesus says that in the Judgment some will say, "Lord, Lord, we have cast out demons and done miracles in your name." Surely these folks, with their treasure trove of good deeds, have accepted Jesus Christ? But Jesus surprises them with, "I don't know you."

I've observed Christians develop near spiritual schizophrenia over this subject. Some—like Judas—look just as good (maybe better?) than others. Nobody knows what they are *really* like until the big crisis hits driving them to perhaps betray even their closest friends.

Then we have people like Peter who say, "Look, you can count on me! Everyone else is going to leave you, but not me!" But only a short time later he abandons Jesus and runs for his life. He also betrays Jesus by cursing and denying that he ever "knew that man."

Judas and Peter: What is the difference?

Consider two trees in the forest, which look strong and secure before the storm. Then, crashing to the ground, one gives evidence of being rotten at the core.

Jesus illustrates this with a story in Matthew 7:24-27 where two men build their dream homes: one on a rock foundation, the other on sand. The storm comes and the strength of each foundation becomes obvious. The point of this story is that neither house can change or deny its foundation during the storm.

Equally true for humans. The metaphorical storms of life openly reveal who or what you have already become. That's it! What a haunting yet simple illustration of Judgment Day.

Those who study behavioral science tell us that every decision made in a crisis is premeditated, meaning that all your life's story before the event has positioned you for when the crisis comes. Life patterns established now determine whether you stand or fall in the tempest that is certain to come.

Judas lost; Peter saved: What was the difference?

Which brings us to the important question: To what kind of person will Jesus say when He returns, "Come inherit the kingdom I've prepared for you"? Answers differ among Christian groups. Both Judas and Peter crashed in the testing. But Judas was lost, Peter saved.

As noted in Chapter Two, Christian viewpoints on salvation generally fall into four groups:
1. Catholic and Orthodox: You will be saved if you do enough of the sacred rituals, i.e. mass, confession, etc.
2. Reformed: God has already chosen who will be saved or lost, irrespective of your choices or lifestyle.
3. All religions where works count for everything.
4. Evangelical: You cannot be lost after accepting Jesus, irrespective of how nasty your life is thereafter.

Do you struggle with any or all of these concepts which seem to minimize logic, free will, and God's grace? I do. While each viewpoint has its merits, my concerns are these:
1. If I'm saved by rituals, then is my willful ongoing sinful lifestyle of no eternal consequence if my quota of rituals is up to date?
2. If God foreordained me to be saved, then how do my choices change that verdict?
3. If I am saved by working hard, how will I ever know if I've done enough?
4. If I cannot be lost after accepting Jesus, then can I revert to my old sinful lifestyle worry-free?

From my extensive biblical study on this topic, I'm suggesting a simpler, more logical and scriptural conclusion: the *Whatever Factor,* based on the Apostle Paul's words in 1 Corinthians 10:31: "WhatEVER I eat or drink or whatEVER I do, I will do it all for the glory of God."

This whatEVER mindset focuses utmost on what matters to God. Paul had a whatEVER attitude as the basis of his confident relationship with Jesus. He not only accepted God's saving grace but also chose a lifestyle that restored God's character in himself. WhatEVER mattered to God also mattered to Paul. As such, he will humbly celebrate God's presence for eternity.

Believers with either of the "whatever" attitudes will fall sooner or later. But as God reads each heart, He knows whether one's attitude is "WHATever" or "whatEVER." As such, the difference between Judas and Peter was that Jesus knew Peter's was a "whatEVER" repentance, even though his immature faith was far from perfect—even after the Resurrection.

Some years ago a fanatic nationalist rushed into the Vatican with a hammer and began smashing Michelangelo's *Pieta*, a marble statue of an anguished Mary holding the crucified Christ. The damage was significant: Mary's lower left arm severed and part of her face smashed. Because this iconic statue was important to Roman Catholic believers, their leaders began asking if this attack on their icon was prophetic of troubles awaiting their church. Quickly the Vatican implored the best available artist to restore the *Pieta* to near perfection. And he did.

In Ephesians 2 the Apostle Paul points out that we are all damaged vessels, desperately needing restoration. "For we are God's workmanship (work of art) and we all are being transformed [back] into His image." 2 Corinthians 3:18

To the Romans, he wrote: "Therefore, do not conform to the pattern of this world, but be transformed by the renewing of your mind." Romans 12:2

Only God can transform His iconic creation masterpiece: you. And He will. This transformation involves both His grace and our faith. It's up to us to decide whether we will enter into this mind-transforming, character-restoring faith relationship.

We make this decision both at our initial conversion—and every day thereafter.

Salvation Compared to Marriage

The Bible compares our saving relationship with Jesus to that of marriage. You don't have a healthy marriage by merely saying "I do" at the altar and, thereafter, developing an "I will live every day to please self" attitude.

A saving relationship with Jesus is more than just saying "I DO accept Jesus as my Lord and Savior." It must then be followed by: "I will seek to live a whatEVER-you-ask" life ever after. A life that pleases Him.

Both faith responses are necessary: 1) I accept Jesus as my Savior, and 2) I daily choose a whatEVER attitude, asking Jesus to transform my mind as I intentionally surrender my life to whatEVER He wishes. The perfect marriage, a living faith.

In Matthew 7: 23 Jesus predicted that in the final Judgment He will say to some poor folks who thought they have done enough good things to be saved, "I never knew you." How do you avoid that disastrous situation where you think you've done enough to be saved yet get the door slammed in your face? The simple answer brings us back to the Whatever Factor.

A WHATever versus a whatEVER Christian

Your eternity hangs on your answer.

A WHATever believer can do many things that outwardly appear to be honoring to God, but inwardly may have a "no big deal" attitude toward some of God's other commands. In contrast, a whatEVER believer, while not perfect, still seeks to have the ATTITUDE of Christ, who said, "I do nothing of my own will, but only the will of my Father."

In other words, whatEVER God instructs me to do I will seek to do. No exceptions. And the way that is accomplished is by making my highest priority that of becoming like Jesus: allowing my mind (character) to be transformed by the power of the Holy Spirit to reflect Jesus' desires and values.

Search your own heart. Are there some things in your life that you say, "I know it's not what Jesus would do or think, but it's no big deal"? That's a WHATever attitude.

Adam and Eve were simply asked to obey God's instruction: Do not eat of that one tree. The serpent responded, "Ah, WHATever. No big deal. Besides, if God is so merciful, He'll overlook one nibbled apple."

The sin was when Adam and Eve chose to switch from being a "whatEVER God commands I will do" person to the no-big-deal way of thinking, as in "I will do WHATever."

The Whatever Factor reveals attitude, a big deal with God. Adam and Eve's WHATever attitude resulted in their expulsion from the Garden of Eden. Not because their sin was so great, but because their attitude was incompatible with living in God's presence.

Many Christians tend to think of some sins as big; some, small. Maybe based on how a particular sin hurts others? Maybe for how much one wishes to commit that sin? But God doesn't concern Himself with big sins or little sins; rather He looks at the heart. **With God, attitude is everything.**

The issue of our faith response to salvation and God's grace is not measured by the number of good things we do nor the number of bad things we avoid. Nor are we judged by our accomplishments or failures.

Instead, *we will be judged according to the character we allow Jesus to form in us.*

That character is demonstrated by one of two "whatever" attitudes. It matters not if you are a believer of only a few hours like the thief on the cross who, if he lived, would have a truck load of sinful patterns that needed transforming. Nor does it matter if you have given 70, 80, 90 years of your life to ministry (like Mother Teresa or Billy Graham) and the sins you still struggle with appear outwardly benign. (Lust of the eye? An unforgiving spirit?)

Perfect or imperfect behaviors do not define your life. Rather, the transformed whatEVER attitude of your soul.

Safe to Save!

Rethink this another way: *Are you safe to save?*

God will not allow a person to enter heaven who nurtures a sin-producing attitude. The WHATever mindset toward ANY of His commands—knowingly and persistently nurtured—rots out the integrity of our soul, producing a WHATever character... which would restart the cosmic sin cycle.

Thus, one sin persistently cherished can and will eventually neutralize all the power of God's grace. That's why James 2:10 says: "For whosoever shall keep the whole law, and yet offend in one point, he is guilty of all." (KJV)

Attitude is everything.

You can't say "I have cancer, but it's only in one lymph node." Hardly. A cancer not quickly eradicated will destroy the whole body. Likewise, a WHATever attitude persistently cherished toward just one command is a metaphorical "sin-cancer" that will eventually neutralize all of God's transformational work in your character... resulting in your loss of salvation.

In Luke 18:8 Jesus said: "When the Son of Man comes, will he find faith on the earth?" I've always wondered what that meant. Could it refer to the Whatever Factor? When Jesus returns, how many people will He find who have a "whatEVER I do, I do for Your glory"?

This whatEVER attitude is implied in other biblical passages: "Then he (Jesus) told all of them, 'If anyone wants to come with me, he must deny himself, pick up his cross every day, and follow me continuously.'" Luke 9:23

King David had the same prayer. "Search me, God, and know my heart... See if there is ANY offensive way in me, and lead me in the way everlasting." Psalm 139:23-24

While you'll never reach absolute perfection this side of heaven, the goal should be, "Lord, I give you control of EVERYTHING today and tomorrow." Today. Tomorrow. Throughout eternity. That's an attitude God cherishes and can transform. THAT person will not only be "safe to save" but also one who will enjoy living in God's presence.

With this understanding, let's reexamine Dr. Stanley's statement:

> Discipleship has nothing to do with whether you will go to heaven or not.... It is possible to be a child of God and never a disciple of Christ.

If someone is not a disciple now, then presumably he is NOT taking up his cross and following Jesus. And, thus, he is not enjoying a continuing fellowship with Jesus and the character transformation that comes with the indwelling of the Holy Spirit. So why would God take him to heaven? (Or her!) Think about it, **why would God force someone to live with Him forever who doesn't enjoy living fully in His will now?** When you know Jesus, you will love Him. When you love Him, you'll passionately embrace a whatEVER attitude and will long to have Him restore His very mind and character in you. That's a heaven-bound believer!

So, how do you get to know Him? Like you get to know anyone else: talk with Him, read and dwell on His love letter to you, unselfishly serve others. Most important, pray for an attitude where you welcome His presence in every activity of your life.

Walking with Jesus Now

Sam Childers, better known as *The Machine Gun Preacher,* spoke at my church on a couple occasions. He shared a personal story that I thought was a good comparison between the WHATever and whatEVER attitude.

Because of his notoriety, and particularly because of his work for the persecuted in Africa, Childers has been a welcome guest at many socials where movie stars, rock stars, and other people of media fame gather. His prayer before such an event is always, "Lord, I know you want to touch someone with your love at this event through me. Open my eyes and speak through me."

So he attends. One event in particular featured the usual hot rock band, glamorous women, handsome men, plastic smiles, and shallow chatter. But Childers felt no nudge by God to engage in any meaningful conversation. Then an astute party-goer approached him. "Sam, I've been watching you. There are a lot of people here who call themselves 'Christian,' but you are the only one who brought Jesus with you to this party."

Yes, just as Childers was ready to leave that party, God nudged him into conversation with a woman who admitted she was there as her last "if this is all there is to life, then break out the booze and have a ball" night before committing suicide.

THAT, is what a "welcome His presence in every activity" attitude looks like: being both a child of God and a disciple of Christ.

The biblical "WhatEVER" attitude fully dignifies your free will and logically ensures your security in God's grace. For when you fall into disobedience while in the process of being transformed back into His image, you will repent. And your repentance will not be the shallow "forgive me for all my sins" variety where you're sorry you got caught or worried about being lost. Rather, your repentance will be heartfelt. After all, you have broken the heart of your best Friend.

Nor will you fear that you might be lost between the moment you stumble and the time you repent. God reads your heart and attitude and always knows the direction you choose to travel, even though you stumble often along the way.

You know that God in His mercy *will* lift you up and, with mercy, say: "I do not condemn you. Now get up and continue your journey of growing your new life in Me. You ARE My child. Because I KNOW your heart, you are secure in My love."

"God does not see the same way people see. People look at the outside of the person, but the LORD looks at the heart." 1 Samuel 16:7 (NCV)

A final thought worthy of reflection from a 19th century author:

> How often our service to Christ, our communion with one another, is marred by the secret desire to exalt self! How ready the thought of self-congratulation, and the longing for human approval! It is the love of self, the desire for an easier way than God has appointed that leads

The "Whatever" Factor

to the substitution of human theories and traditions for the divine precepts. When the faith we accept destroys selfishness and pretense, when it leads us to seek God's glory and not our own, we may know that it is of the right order.[10]

Faith that is "of the right order"? Faith that "leads us to seek God's glory? That can only be the whatEVER kind!

---

[10] From *Desire of Ages, p. 409 by E.G. White.*

Imagination Station #1

"Who wants to go to heaven?" The Sunday school teacher put that question to her classroom of boys and girls, All the children shot their hands into the air. Except Johnny. He sat there, wavering, sullen, puzzled.

"Johnny?" the teacher said. "Do you NOT want to go to heaven?"

"Well, I guess I do," he said, glum as a captured truant.

"Then why didn't you put up your hand?"

"Because my mom made chocolate cake for dinner tonight. I was really hoping to have some."

In 1970 as part of my master's degree training I taught a senior religion class at a Christian high school. I asked them the same question and got a mixed response. Then I asked what would be the most enjoyable thing they might do in heaven. Their #1 answer? "Ride a lion."

*I have no doubt that riding a lion would be a thrill, at least for the first couple of times. But heaven is **forever!** But how about after ten or twenty rides?*

The question I like to ask believers is: What are you going to do in heaven... after the first couple months?

So, what is your concept of heaven? Our perception of our goal must be enticing enough to stir our passionate commitment assuring that the journey we're on does, in fact, culminate in heaven's glory.

Following each chapter in these "Imagination Stations" I will attempt to awaken you to the exciting possibilities heaven may hold.

Chapter 2:

Sincerely Uncertain About Assurance

"So, you were ALL half right. But I love you anyway." God

Perhaps you've heard the story.

The redeemed saints are gathered before the throne of the Almighty—each in their familiar denominational huddle: Baptists, Presbyterians, Lutherans, Mormons, Catholics, Seventh-day Adventists, Pentecostals, Methodists... and the non-denominationals drifting amongst all the groups sharing hugs.

What will be the first words they hear from the Almighty on the throne? "Well done, good and faithful servants" would be biblical. Or perhaps the Father would preface that with, "You know, saints, I have some bad news and some good news. Which would you like to hear first?"

A Minnesota Lutheran shouts, "Give us the bad news."

"Okay, as you wish. The bad news is that all of you were wrong in some things."

The huddlers stir and murmur. From the Almighty, that's a bit unsettling. The non-denoms, however, nod and smile: "That's what we've been saying all along!"

"But," continues the Holy One, "the good news is that I love you anyway. And you *each* did a few things very well."

Moral: Heaven is likely to have its surprises!

I was reared in and for the first thirty-four years of ministry I served in a denomination that believed its theology to be more biblically correct than any other religious group. And perhaps it was. However, as if to balance my resume, during the next nine years I founded and pastored a nondenominational church where we willingly embraced the idea that God shared his grace within and through whatever group was available for God's Spirit to use in any given time and place, irrespective of denominational label.

I'm not an expert on each denomination, but life and ministry have allowed me the privilege of becoming familiar with many. Most groups purport to have the best grasp of biblical truths. That's why they are where they are! And "membership" within that particular group is important for self-validation and self-identity.

Exceptions exist. Many of the non-denoms have a much more inclusive attitude AND some of the liberal Protestant main-line churches are much more ecumenically minded wherein their uniqueness as a denomination seems to carry a more historical (rather than doctrinal) importance.

But there are some beliefs that multiple groups hold in common, one being: "For by grace you have been saved through faith." Ephesians 2:8 (RSV)

Admitting up front that I may be guilty of oversimplification (so please forgive me if I don't fully portray your theology), many Christian churches who teach "salvation by grace through faith" differ as to *how* this saving grace is dispensed. Typically, they embrace one or more of the following:

GRACE: dispensed through participation in holy rituals

Some churches, such as Roman Catholicism, teach that one important way grace is acquired and dispensed is through the believer's participation in holy rituals, i.e. Mass, Eucharist, prayers or pilgrimages to that church's designated holy sites.

On the subject of the Catholic Mass, this example is found (*Catholicculture.org*):

> The Mass is the divinely ordained means of applying the merits of Calvary. Christ won for the world all the graces it needs for salvation and sanctification. But these blessings are conferred gradually and continually since Calvary and mainly through the Mass. Their measure of conferral is in proportion to the faith and loving response of the faithful who unite themselves in spirit with the Mass.

More so in years past, the Roman Catholic Church exerted controlling power over its congregants by threatening excommunication if they misbehaved. Thus, by barring their members' attendance from Mass, the necessary grace dispensed through the Eucharist was believed to be withheld.

An example of the Catholic concept of dispensing grace through other holy rituals would be The Holy Stairs located opposite the Basilica of San Giovanni Laterano in Rome. According to Catholic tradition, these twenty-eight marble steps (now protected by wooden boards) were part of the Praetorium of Pilate in Jerusalem which Jesus ascended during his Passion. Medieval legends claim that The Holy Stairs were brought from Jerusalem to Rome about 326 AD by Helena, mother of Constantine the Great. Traditionally, pilgrims are eager to ascend The Holy Stairs on their knees, reciting prescribed prayers, for a promise of nine years of indulgences (dispensed grace which gives them reprieve from the fires of Purgatory) for each step they climb.

Samuele Bacchiocchi, a doctoral student at the Pontifical Gregorian University in Rome from 1969 to 1974, worked occasionally as a tour guide in the Vatican. On one occasion, as he escorted his group to The Holy Stairs, an American tourist asked the attending priest: "Please, Father, could you explain to me what will happen if I ascend The Holy Stairs in the prescribed manner four times, earning a total of 1008 years of indulgences, but I need only 500 years of indulgence to transit from purgatory to paradise? What is God going to do with the 508 extra years of indulgence that I worked for?" The priest, responding in a pastoral manner, assured him: "My son, do not worry about the extra indulgences, because God will automatically apply them to your relatives in purgatory."

This experience illustrates how the fear of purgatory and/or hell has historically motivated pious Catholics to undertake pilgrimages to "holy shrines," to perform disciplines like ascending The Holy Stairs, fasting, alms giving, the recitation of prayers for the dead, and even to pay for memorial masses—all in the hope of shortening the temporal punishment in purgatory for themselves and/or loved ones.

This reminds me of story recited by a new member of my congregation when I pastored my first church in Southern California in 1974. She was in her thirties and the previous year had left the Catholic faith to join our church. Her Catholic mother, who lived less than a holy life, pled with her daughter, "If you leave the Roman Catholic faith, then who will pray my soul out of purgatory?"

Although never a member of the Catholic faith, I had the privilege in 1969 of visiting Notre Dame University in South Bend, Indiana. While on the campus I walked the Trail of Memories, where I stopped at the Grotto of Lourdes and the old Log Chapel. At the entrance of both were plaques informing the Catholic member that their visit to these holy sites earned them several hundred days of dispensed grace from the tortures of purgatory.

Although purgatory is seldom a topic of interest in current Western Catholic teaching, the concept of dispensed grace through participation in holy rituals is still taught in many parts of the world. But questions arise:
- How do I know for a certainty that I have visited enough holy sites, attended enough masses and cited enough of the correct prayers?
- Can I be saved if I am zealously faithful in the rites while remaining mean and selfish or an unrepentant adulterer, drunkard, or pedophile?

Who can know?

GRACE: dispensed only to those whom God chooses

Typically this conversation would take place with someone of the reformed Protestant faith under the topic of "God's election."

As Matt Slick, President and Founder of the Christian Apologetics and Research Ministry, explains on his *www.carm.org* web site:

Predestination and election are both Biblical teachings... The Reformed doctrine of predestination is that God predestines whom He wants to be saved and that without this predestination, none would be saved. The non-Reformed camp states that God predestines people to salvation but that these people freely choose to follow God on their own. In other words, in the non-Reformed perspective God is reacting to the will of individuals and predestining them only because they choose God where by contrast the Reformed position states that people choose God only because He has first predestined them.

Although this theology puts a high premium on the sovereignty of God, it too raises legitimate questions:

- If God pre-ordains who will be saved, then does my accepting of Jesus Christ really matter? Am I forced or manipulated into choosing God?
- Why should my salvation concern me if that decision is out of my control?
- If I am one of the lucky "elect," will I be saved in spite of my lifestyle?

Interesting questions that, again, are difficult to answer.

GRACE: dispensed through belief in correct doctrine

In the Middle Ages, both Protestants and Catholics labeled people with beliefs that differed from theirs as "heretics," often with painful consequences. Many heretics were tortured and/or killed. The belief was that if the church's henchmen inflicted enough pain upon the heretic, hopefully the deceived soul would renounce his false beliefs and receive salvation. Sounds preposterous, but true.

Today, torturing heretics is not in vogue, at least in the Christian world. But church groups still express their "saved by correct doctrine" in more subtle ways. For example, couples with different denominational backgrounds are often forbidden to marry because "the unbelieving spouse might lead our son or daughter astray." Christians of another label might be called *outsiders* or, using a more traditional term, *apostates*. A member who leaves one denomination for another might be called a *backslider, unbeliever, unorthodox,* or *deceived*.

The underlying premise to this thinking is: "If you believe THAT, then you cannot be saved because that teaching is a misrepresentation of the Almighty and an affront to His holiness." Thus, by implication, an incorrect doctrine forfeits saving grace.

Questions arise here as well:
- How do I really know that what I believe IS correct doctrine?

- Will I know because so many Godly teachers and preachers believe the same?
- Will I know by a burning sensation in my breast—as a Mormon might suggest? Or do I know because I am given some other sign?
- And what if my beloved teacher changes his interpretation or the sign was merely a coincidence, wishful thinking—or *heartburn*?

Have you ever believed something to be 100% true only to discover years later that the doctrine was only partially correct—or totally off the mark?

Which brings us back to my opening story. Imagine God's sympathetic gaze and smile as He whispers, "So, you were *all* half right! But I love you anyway."

GRACE: dispensed through holy living

Belief in "grace through correct doctrine" may govern your theology under eligibility for grace.

For example, some folks who believe that the seventh-day is the only true Sabbath might say, "The fourth commandment requires one to observe the seventh-day Sabbath; therefore, all who knowingly disregard this commandment by worshiping on Sunday will be lost." They would call attention to Revelation 14:12 (NKJV) and say that both faith AND obedience are necessary prerequisites to receiving saving grace: "Here is the patience of the saints; here are those who keep the commandments (including the seventh-day Sabbath) of God and the faith of Jesus."

Those emphasizing this faith-plus-works theology will say that "faith without works is dead," citing Romans 2:14-26 (NIV):

> What good is it, my brothers and sisters, if someone claims to have faith but has no deeds?

Can such faith save them? Suppose a brother or a sister is without clothes and daily food. If one of you says to them, "Go in peace; keep warm and well fed," but does nothing about their physical needs, what good is it? In the same way, faith by itself, if it is not accompanied by action, is dead.

But someone will say, "You have faith; I have deeds."

Show me your faith without deeds, and I will show you my faith by my deeds. You believe that there is one God. Good! Even the demons believe that—and shudder.

You foolish person, do you want evidence that faith without deeds is useless? Was not our father Abraham considered righteous for what he did when he offered his son Isaac on the altar? You see that his faith and his actions were working together, and his faith was made complete by what he did. And the scripture was fulfilled that says, 'Abraham believed God, and it was credited to him as righteousness,' and he was called God's friend. You see that a person is considered righteous by what they do and not by faith alone.

In the same way, was not even Rahab the prostitute considered righteous for what she did when she gave lodging to the spies and sent them off in a different direction? As the body without the spirit is dead, so faith without deeds is dead.

Sincerely Uncertain About Assurance

Many conclude that grace is forfeited for both not believing AND practicing correct doctrine.

The concern here is:
- How do I know if I've done enough good deeds to be worthy of God's saving grace?
- We all know we fall short of the "glory of God," but how short can I fall and still be saved?
- Do I need to be "perfect, even as your Father which is in heaven is perfect?" Matthew 5:38 (KJV)

During my years of denominational pastoring, I often heard this concern expressed in public prayer: "And Lord, when you come in the clouds of glory may we be found *worthy* to enter into eternal live." The implication is that today we probably aren't worthy of salvation but, maybe... hopefully... we will eventually be worthy.

Does being "worthy" come via advanced age or tribulation or by my increased intensity of fasting and prayer? And how will I know if I've done enough?

Again, who can answer?

GRACE: irretrievably dispensed merely by confession of belief in Jesus Christ

All Christian faith groups teach that belief in Christ is a necessary element of salvation.

Sure, some will add:

"Believe in Christ and attend Mass to be saved."

Or, "believe in Christ and hold correct doctrines."

Or, "believe in Christ and live a holy life."

But a large number of Evangelicals teach this: "Accept Jesus Christ as your Lord and Savior, be baptized, and you can never be lost—regardless of your lifestyle or faith after your confession."

In other words, saving grace is forever guaranteed by just once reciting the rite of confessing belief in Jesus Christ AND being truly sincere about your confession. This is called "security-of-salvation." Adherents to this belief quote the Apostle Paul from Acts 16:25-34 (NKJV):

> But at midnight Paul and Silas were praying and singing hymns to God, and the prisoners were listening to them. Suddenly there was a great earthquake, so that the foundations of the prison were shaken; and immediately all the doors were opened and everyone's chains were loosed. And the keeper of the prison, awaking from sleep and seeing the prison doors open, supposing the prisoners had fled, drew his sword and was about to kill himself. But Paul called with a loud voice, saying, "Do yourself no harm, for we are all here."
>
> Then he called for a light, ran in, and fell down trembling before Paul and Silas. And he brought them out and said, "Sirs, what must I do to be saved?"
>
> So they said, "Believe on the Lord Jesus Christ, and you will be saved, you and your household." Then they spoke the word of the Lord to him and to all who were in his house. And he took them the same hour of the night and washed their stripes. And immediately he and all his family were baptized. Now when he had brought them into his house, he set food before them; and he rejoiced, having believed in God with all his household.

The Security-Gospel Christians find assurance in Philippians 1:3-6 (NKJV):

> I thank my God upon every remembrance of you, always in every prayer of mine making request for you all with joy, for your fellowship in the gospel from the first day until now, being confident of this very thing, that He who has begun a good work in you will complete it until the day of Jesus Christ.

Another supporting passage is 2 Corinthians 1:20-22 (NKJV):

> For all the promises of God in Him are Yes and in Him Amen, to the glory of God through us. Now He who establishes us with you in Christ and has anointed us is God, who also has sealed us and given us the Spirit in our hearts as a guarantee.

Don't misunderstand: I know of no Evangelical who teaches that once you have accepted Jesus you can live any old way you want. In fact, many Evangelical groups have historically been in the forefront of holiness movements whereby disciplined holy behavior is expected and often demanded.[11]

But why their emphasis on holy living? Most who adhere to the security-of-salvation persuasion would say that the natural response to knowing that Jesus died for their salvation is to

---

[11] Wikipedia defines this concept in this manner: "The holiness movement refers to a set of beliefs and practices emerging from 19th-century Methodism, and to a number of evangelical Christian denominations who emphasize those beliefs as a central doctrine. The movement is distinguished by its emphasis on John Wesley's "Christian perfection" teaching—the belief that it is possible to live free of voluntary sin, and particularly by the belief that this may be accomplished instantaneously through a second work of grace."

express one's gratitude by holy living. Plus, holy living can be a witness to the power of Jesus to change lives. But their greatest motivation seems to be the belief that heavenly rewards are doled out in proportion to the believer's level of holy living. (We'll look at this concept more in Section IV.)

The sincerity of their belief in the holy life has, unfortunately, often produced a very judgmental attitude toward other members who don't seem to "take their religion seriously" and, thus, are subjected to harsh church discipline. In spite of this zeal for holy living, their doctrine of "you can never be lost if you have sincerely accepted Jesus" means that lack of piety can never put one's salvation in jeopardy.

A Belief that Is Believable!

I'm quite certain that adherents of any one of these above noted belief systems would bemoan my brief and (in their perception) incomplete depiction of their theology. No doubt many more texts on both sides of the discussion could be noted and discussed, but the question essentially remains the same: How DO you know that you are on the road to eternal life?

Even if you believe that irrevocable grace is dispensed when you sincerely accepted Jesus Christ as Lord and Savior, then how do you know you were adequately sincere?

On all sides there is much doubt and fear. The truth is, Satan is happy regardless of the side folks choose as long as they miss an accurate understanding of how God relates to us and how He wants us to relate to Him.

Join me in focusing on the assurance of salvation through a new and completely biblical lens: the "Whatever Factor."

The "Whatever Factor" bridges the theology of all the groups regarding salvation. God doesn't want us to dwell merely on the beginning or the end of our spiritual journey. He wants us to primarily focus and live with Him, in His presence, in the now.

Through our current relationship with Him, we allow God to transform our character and reveal whether we are heaven bound. The beauty of the "Whatever Factor" attitude is that it doesn't stop at the Second Coming of Jesus: it continues throughout eternity. So in essence, we are living in eternity now.

In the next few chapters, let's explore this idea both simply and deeply. No stone unturned. And because it's true, it's all Good News!

Imagination Station #2

We all have a high level of anticipation for those first months inside heaven's gates including:
- *Hug Jesus and our departed loved ones and friends*
- *Ask those questions that have always troubled us*
- *Sing our hearts out with the angel choir at some worship services around God's throne*
- *Investigate the streets of gold*
- *Check out the new home Jesus has prepared*
- *Taste the fruit from the Tree of Life*
- *Wade in the River of Life*
- *Test our flying skills*

Then what? Forever is a long, LONG time.

First, let's discuss what we know about heaven from the Bible's description. Later then, we'll stretch our imagination as to what heaven **could be**.

We know that heaven is where the pain stops. In Revelation 21:4 we read: "He will wipe every tear from their eyes. There will be no more death or mourning or crying or pain, for the old order of things has passed away."

If you are a tortured and terrorized victim of oppression and war—or simply suffer from arthritis, diabetes, or loneliness—then this promise is huge. In every Christian funeral that I've conducted, this text of hope is read. Because all of us are victims of pain and death.

For many, heaven will be **relief.**

Chapter 3:

Isn't Sincerity at the Altar Enough?

"Even if a believer for all practical purposes becomes an unbeliever, his salvation is not in jeopardy."
Dr. Charles Stanley, *Eternal Security*, p. 93.

If Stanley is correct, then there will be unbelievers in heaven. Maybe that's what preachers mean when they talk about God's mind-blowing, scandalous grace. But is it grace to take someone to heaven who doesn't really want to be there? Food for thought.

In the 1999 James Bond spy thriller *The World Is Not Enough*, Bond is tasked with protecting the wealthy and powerful oil mistress, Elektra King, against an expected assassin. The story takes a dramatic turn when 007 discovers that Elektra IS the terrorist mastermind plotting to control the world through oil manipulation. At their final confrontation in her tower, she offers him the world if he will join her in the dastardly scheme. His response is the movie's ultimate punch line: "The world is not enough!"

The reflective question in the viewer's mind could be, "So what IS enough?"

Regarding salvation security, the question is: *What is enough?* Some believers would say, "Work harder to be worthy of salvation." But others say that pure grace takes people to heaven if they have a "feeling" that they accepted Jesus with adequate sincerity.

I once had a minister of music who embraced the security-of-salvation belief: "Accept Jesus as your Lord and Savior and you are guaranteed salvation... no matter what. Period." She directed my attention to biblical passages that say God will "keep us" and not let us out of His hand.

We often enjoyed cordial—but spirited—discussions about this belief. One day I asked her if God would force a Christian to heaven whose later life was both a denial and an abomination to Christ. She answered, "No, God wouldn't take that person to heaven because that rebellious attitude shows that he was never truly converted in the first place."

"So," I asked, "how do you know that you are truly converted and won't do the same?"

Her reply? "I just know."

After a pause, I felt compelled to respond. "I've worked with some folks who were as serious as can be when they made their initial decision to accept Jesus, yet they later threw in the towel. So how do you know for certain that you were sincere enough when you walked forward to the altar to accept Jesus?"

"I just do."

"So is your assurance that you will not reject Christ later in life wholly based on some feeling of *just knowing* you were sincere enough when you accepted Jesus?"

The conversation stalled. What had started out as a discussion of guaranteed salvation by accepting Christ got a bit wobbly when it boiled down to a feeling of "just knowing." How can one *really* know he or she were sincere enough? And again, what is *enough?*

Isn't Sincerity at the Altar Enough?

Without trying to diminish fellow pastors, I've often thought: It's unfortunate that Evangelical ministers in their seminary training don't receive a Sincerity Meter as a graduation gift. They could use it at every altar call. Each person coming forward to accept Jesus Christ would put their hand on the meter pad and immediately know if their sincerity met the salvation standard.

Sincerity can be so genuine, yet so temporary. I've officiated at scores of marriage altars where I've heard couples say "I do" in the deepest sincerity—and they really meant it. However, a few years later, half were sincerely certain that their marriage was not working and divorce imminent. That Sincerity Meter could come in handy in these settings as well. Just before asking, "Is there anyone who objects to the union of this man to this woman?" the minister could check the meter. If the red light flashed, then the marriage announcement could be aborted and many future divorces avoided.

We simply do not know our own hearts. "The heart is fooled more than anything else, and is very sinful. Who can know how bad it is?" Jeremiah 17:9 (NLV) To base one's salvation on "just knowing" that you were sincere enough at your conversion is at best a wish and a hope. Not much better, actually, than those poor folks who believe they will be saved if they become "worthy enough." When the "worthy enough" group is asked if they're saved, they often respond, "I hope so." But those who believe they're irrevocably saved at conversion when asked if they are certain that their conversion was sincere enough might answer the same: "I hope so. I felt really sincere."

Or, they could respond with a nebulous, "I just know."

Other uncomfortable questions arise. After accepting Jesus, if a person were to slip away—or boldly and defiantly stalk away—and engage in the worst sort of decadent and destructive behavior the rest of his life (such that in his atheistic dying breath he cursed God), would he still be saved? Will God take him to heaven against his will? Like a child who is angrily writhing and screaming in protest as his father totes him away from the candy counter, will God drag someone to heaven, who is screaming "I hate you! I hate you!" because earlier in her life she confessed the Lord Jesus Christ as Lord and Savior?

Why These Questions Matter

Some Evangelical writers would say that these questions are irrelevant, taking the stance that a sincerely converted Christian cannot fall away. Clark Whitten, in his popular book *Pure Grace* says this:

> It is impossible for a true Christian—one who has become a new creation in Christ, one who has been raised from spiritual death to life, one who is the righteousness of God in Christ—to ever reject Christ or ever disbelieve His divinity. Impossible! I have never met one person like that, and neither have you because they do not exist.... True Christians are one spirit with Christ and could never reject Him. It is simply impossible!
>
> Any person who can reject Christ, stop believing, or plunge into a life of rebellion against God without remorse, was simply never born again—regardless of testimony to the contrary. True Christians cannot deny Jesus, and true unbelievers cannot remain with Him.[12]

Regarding Pastor Whitten's first point, I cannot question whether he has "never" met a person who experienced new life in Christ but eventually gave up their faith. But I believe his

---
[12] *Pure Grace* by Clark Whitten, Destiny Image Publishers 2012, pg. 130.

statement is more of a wish than a fact. The reality for most of us is that we DO know people who, once passionate about their faith, later became either agnostics or atheists.

The causes are legion: unanswered faith questions that went from doubt to unbelief. Or the old life of sin and vice reasserted its ugly head. Or they faced terrible pain and suffering that led them to believe that there is not a loving God: worst case scenarios being the evil and insanity of war, internment in a concentration camp, or prolonged sexual abuse. In each of these scenarios some have lost their faith in God because their prayers went unanswered and evil seemed to triumph.

If one's eyes are open, it is not difficult to find people who once sincerely believed the Gospel, but eventually denied their faith.

The Danger of Irrevocable Grace

In response to Whitten's second point, the idea that a "true Christian cannot deny Jesus" seems a bit utopian. In fact it could be dangerous to the believer. How so?

Let's say Michelle had a sincere conversion at age thirteen. For years thereafter she is a model spiritual leader—both in her own heart and in the view of many others. Then the dark side of life tackles her. She goes to an Ivy League University where her atheistic professors challenge her with questions about creation, God's existence, and the issue of suffering. Her faith is unsettled because previous answers seem so naive.

Then she is a victim of date rape. She had prayed for God's protection, so how could this happen? She finds a "good Christian" boy and feels secure until she discovers that he evilly entraps young ladies. Feeling betrayed and victimized, she prays more diligently and claims Bible promises like Psalm chapters 23 and 91 where the believer is assured God's deliverance from evil.

The walls of her soul are closing in: her faith questioned by her professors, her purity gone. Under the dangerous spell of a sadistic boyfriend, she goes to a pastor for counseling. He's good. Very good. In fact, she ends up in bed with the pastor before she knows what happened.

Her spiritual world has imploded. At that point she is haunted by the *big* doubts: "Here I am wrestling with my faith and God's existence. So if it's impossible for a truly converted person to deny Christ like I read in *Pure Grace,* was I truly converted? Maybe not. If I were God, I would have answered my prayers and all of this bad stuff would not be happening. I thought I was converted, but I must not have been."

Michelle is at a critical intersection in her life. She could take the path away from God because the Bible promises didn't prevent evil from assaulting her world. As Whitten says: "Any person who can reject Christ, stop believing, or plunge into a life of rebellion against God without remorse, was simply never born again."

Turning away from her faith, I wonder if Michelle might not cry out: "So maybe the Reformed Calvinists are right. I was not one of God's elect. My conversion was a sick comedy!" The last thing a Christ-follower needs to worry about is that her conversion was a charade.

It *is* possible for a sincere follower of God to turn away. That's why the New Testament writers continually warn believers to be on guard lest they "fall away" from Christ.

Read the Fine Print

Like every marketing offer of desirable goods offered at minimal cost, let's look at the qualifiers (the fine print, if you will) of Whitten's statement. He claims: "It is impossible for a true Christian—*one who has become a new creation in Christ, one who has been raised from spiritual death to life, one who is the righteousness of God in Christ*—to ever reject Christ."

Isn't Sincerity at the Altar Enough?

This statement goes way beyond a "sincere confession of faith in Jesus" that most Evangelicals embrace as a ticket to heaven. Notice that he says it is impossible for a believer to reject Christ if they have already, first, "*become a new creation in Christ.*" Does he mean in theory—or reality? In theory, according to Paul in 2 Corinthians 5:17, all believers are declared to be new creatures in Christ. That is our new standing before God, but it's not yet a daily reality with all our fleshly stuff to yet deal with.

Paul recognizes this huge gap between a person being pronounced a new creature versus reality when writing to the Roman believers: "Count yourselves dead to sin but alive to God in Christ Jesus. Therefore do not let sin reign in your mortal body so that you obey its evil desires." Romans 6:11-12. In other words, since you are declared to be a new creature who has died to sin and been resurrected into Jesus' likeness, then stop allowing sin to control you and start acting like God's new creation!

Let's apply Paul's counsel to marriage. A couple days after your wedding you remember the biblical line from your wedding: the "two of you have become one." But it's going to take a lifetime of loving, forgiving, compromising and patience to become one in heart, mind and soul. None of us have yet become—in our emotions, thoughts, choices and actions—that "new creation" in Christ. The model held before us takes a lifetime of pressing toward that goal.

Whitten's second qualifier is the phrase "*been raised from spiritual death to life.*" Again, theory or reality? Paul's warning to the Romans indicates that the spiritual transformation from "death to life" is a work of a lifetime.

In the marriage vows, each party promises "till death do us part, to serve each other through sickness/health, rich/poor," etc. But all newlyweds discover (some even on their honeymoon!) that they have NOT totally died to self. That work has just begun.

And last, Whitten includes, "[O]ne who is the righteousness of God in Christ." In theory—or in our standing before God? In standing before God, one's sinful life is now covered by the perfect righteousness of Jesus. He or she is declared righteous. But in reality, we are far from righteous in our thoughts, attitudes and actions. That is the lifetime work of opening our minds to the transforming power of the Holy Spirit. As Paul wrote: "Speaking the truth in love, we will grow to become in every respect the mature body of him who is the head, that is, Christ, so that we *grow up in the fullness of the stature of Jesus Christ.*" Ephesians 4:15 [Emphasis mine and all verses in bold throughout this chapter.]

Either Whitten's three qualifiers are true in both theory AND reality, or his bold statement, "It is impossible for a true Christian to ever reject Christ," is false. So I ask: Have you ever met a person who was totally dead to sin and 100% committed to Christ? One whose every attitude, thought, and action reflected the "new creature" status, completely grown up into the fullness of the stature of Jesus Christ? *That* person I personally have never seen.

To think and act like a person totally dead to sin, whose character is fully transformed to reflect the "stature of Jesus Christ" (or we could say "perfectly reflects Christ's mind and character"), is a human who doesn't exist. Rather, Paul teaches that it is our goal. But even Paul had not grown into "the stature of Jesus Christ" as noted in Philippians 3:10-14 (MSG):

> I gave up all that inferior stuff so I could know Christ personally, experience his resurrection power, be a partner in his suffering, and go all the way with him to death itself. If there was any way to get in on the resurrection from the dead, I wanted to do it.

> **I'm not saying that I have this all together,** that I have it made. But **I am well on my way,** reaching out for Christ, who has so wondrously reached out for me. Friends, don't get me wrong: By no means do I count myself an expert in all of this, but **I've got my eye on the goal,** where God is beckoning us onward—to Jesus." [Emphasis mine]

So let's return to our first question: If salvation is ultimately based on a feeling of a "sincere" acceptance of Jesus Christ, can you be assured that the sincerity of your current conviction will last throughout the end of your life? Whitten attempts to answer that question with two texts.

First, Romans 8:38-39: "For I am convinced that neither death nor life, neither angels nor demons, neither the present nor the future, nor any powers, neither height nor depth, nor anything else in all creation, will be able to separate us from the love of God that is in Christ Jesus our Lord."

But wait a minute. The text says that nothing can separate us from the love of God. That is true. We can do nothing to cause God to stop loving us. God loves all sinners—even those who are lost. In fact, He weeps over losing them like a parent over a rebellious child. Nothing can stop God from loving you!

But God's love is not the issue in salvation. The dispute is whether *our love for God* is deep, lasting, and unchangeable. Do "saved" Christians still have control of their choices which might allow Satan to distract and destroy their love for God? Paul's answer is: definitely. We maintain control of our freedom of choice after conversion; as such, Satan will do all in his power to lure us away from God. For Paul himself (and he prayed the same for his readers), this passage is expressing his determination to allow *nothing* to draw him away from God's love.

This determination is noted in Paul's rallying cry of encouragement: "In all these things we are more than conquerors through him who loved us." This appeal is essentially the same as Paul's Philippians 3 challenge, which is that if you want to make sure that your love for God will never fail, then consider yourselves dead to sin and resurrected/alive to Jesus Christ. Then act like it!

Whitten's second text is 1 John 2:19-20: "They went out from us, but they were not really of us; for if they had been of us, they would have remained with us; but they went out so that it would be shown that they all are not of us. But you have an anointing from the Holy One, and **you all know**." Herein lies the heart of his salvation theology: "and you all know." Know *what*, I ask.

Whitten seems to imply that John's readers will "know" that they are God's saved children in contrast to those who left the faith, having never really belonged. But is that really John's point? No. Read the rest of the passage:

> Dear children, this is the last hour; and as you have heard that the antichrist is coming, even now many antichrists have come. This is how we know it is the last hour. They went out from us, but they did not really belong to us. For if they had belonged to us, they would have remained with us; but their going showed that none of them belonged to us. But you have an anointing from the Holy One, and all of you know [Note: This is where Whitten ends John's statement mid-sentence without adding the next two important words] **the truth.** I do not write to you because you do not know the truth, but because you do know it and because no lie comes from the truth. Who is the liar? It

is whoever **denies that Jesus is the Christ**. 1 John 2:18-22 (NIV)

What does John say they *know*? The **truth** that Jesus is the Christ! I find it revealing that the editors of the *New International Version* have placed this heading just above verse 18: "Warnings against denying the Son." Evidently, the editors understand what Whitten does not (or chooses to omit) that John's appeal wasn't about knowing if one's salvation is secure. Instead, this passage teaches: You know the **truth about Jesus Christ**, so I trust that you will not fall for the lies of the antichrist and deny your faith in Christ. . . as others have!

A Warning Signifies a Threat

Simplicity can elicit the clearest truth. *Warnings are issued only if there is a genuine threat.* If Paul's and John's readers were secure in their salvation, then why waste the pen and paper (papyrus, parchment?) warning them of something that could NEVER affect them? If it was impossible for them to be lost, then why the warnings to the contrary? Why would John warn his readers to be on guard against denying Christ if they were secure in their salvation and impossible for them to separate themselves from a God of love?

I can hear it now. "Well, pastor, maybe these antichrists were trying to convince the believers that they were not secure in their salvation and the apostles were trying to remind them that they had nothing to fear."

If that were true, all Paul and John needed to say was: "You accepted Jesus. You can never be lost. Next question?"

More to Salvation than Confession of Faith

Another key question follows: *Isn't sincerity at the altar enough?*

As seen in our study, it should be evident that the Bible clearly says that there is more to salvation than one-time conversion—a momentary confession of faith.

First, let's look at a definition of "security-of-salvation" from one of its proponents:

> The Bible teaches that everyone who is born again by the power of the Holy Spirit is saved forever. We receive the gift of eternal life (John 10:28), not temporary life. Someone who is born again (John 3:3) cannot be "unborn." After being adopted into God's family (Romans 8:15), we will not be kicked out. When God starts a work, He finishes it (Philippians 1:6). So, the child of God—the believer in Jesus Christ—is eternally secure in his salvation.
>
> An apostate is someone who abandons his religious faith. It is clear from the Bible that apostates are people who made professions of faith in Jesus Christ but never genuinely received Him as Savior. They were pretend believers. Those who turn away from Christ never really trusted Him to begin with, as 1 John 2:19 says, 'They went out from us, but they did not really belong to us. For if they had belonged to us, they would have remained with us; but their going showed that none of them belonged to us.' Those who apostatize are simply demonstrating that they are not true believers, and they never were. *www.GotQuestions.org.*

Consider this popular—but inaccurate—security-of-salvation summary:

1. A person who is genuinely sincere at his or her conversion can never be lost.
2. If they later abandon their faith, it shows that they were never genuinely sincere at their conversion.
3. As Dr. Charles Stanley states, even if they were to abandon their faith after a sincere conversion, they cannot be lost.

Evangelical Preachers Do Have Differing Viewpoints

Let's review what appears to be two contradictory Evangelical lines of logic as noted in the above summary.

Students of this topic should be aware that Evangelical writers have divergent views concerning whether a "true Christian" can deny Christ. Whitten says, "True Christians cannot deny Jesus." On the other hand Dr. Charles Stanley's writes: "Even if a believer for all practical purposes becomes an unbeliever, his salvation is not in jeopardy."

Trying to harmonize these opposing viewpoints is like saying, "If a married couple truly loves each other, then neither of them will ever commit adultery (Whitten), BUT even if they did commit adultery it doesn't prove that they didn't love each other (Stanley)." Isn't that nothing more than double talk?

Whitten says that a person who lives an ungodly life after conversion is merely showing that his conversion was never sincere and thus invalid. The opposing concept offered by Stanley implies that if a person (who we assume had a sincere conversion) turns bad, then God will still take them to heaven as an unrepentant and unbelieving person (or perhaps God will manipulate their mind so they will come back to faith before they die). Both agree that a sincere believer will be saved, but one says it is impossible for them to stray, while the other suggests that straying is a possibility.

Such explanations raise several troubling questions:

The Whatever Factor

1. How do you know your conversion was sincere enough to keep you from going rogue?
2. How does God bring you back to faith without manipulating your free will?
3. And if you don't come back to faith, will He take you to heaven anyway?

The second troubling fallacy is offered by Stanley's statement that even if you were to remain an unbeliever to death, your salvation is not in jeopardy, since *"Christ will not deny an unbelieving Christian his or her salvation because to do so would be to deny Himself."*[13] (Implication: you are deserving of salvation merely as His child.)

The questions this raises are even more troubling. If a person dies in a state of unbelief, denial, or antagonism toward God, then:

1. Does God miraculously change that unbelieving person's attitude and character *en route* to heaven, so they will actually enjoy it up there?
2. If no miraculous attitude adjustment takes place, then how would that person enjoy heaven and Jesus—a place and a Person they didn't enjoy at the time of their death?
3. Will these be the folks that Stanley says will be in the "outer darkness" area of heaven where there will be "weeping and gnashing of teeth?"[14]

Which is it? Could a sincere person after conversion ever abandon his or her faith? Do all professed Christians who later abandon their faith prove that they were not sincere at their conversion? Even IF they were to abandon faith (after their sincere

---

[13] *Eternal Security, pg. 94.*

[14] We'll discuss this more in the chapter "The Dark Side of Heaven." Stanley's words were: *"To be in the 'outer darkness' is to be in the kingdom of God but outside the circle of men and women whose faithfulness on this earth earned them a special rank or position of authority."*

conversion), is it impossible for them to be lost? If a person is taken to heaven who died with an antagonistic attitude toward God, how would they find heaven an enjoyable place?

So, returning to the discussion with my minister of music. The implied follow-up conversation could have been: If you were sincere enough at your conversion, will God keep you from straying? Or, might God let you stray "for a season," guaranteeing that He will bring you back into belief before your death?

If either of these assertions is true, then does God remove our free will at the point of our conversion? Does a sincere conversion mean that one is incapable of choosing to stray? Or does it mean that a person could choose to stray, but God would manipulate circumstances such that he or she would choose to repent and return?

I think many Evangelicals would say "Yes, God will find a way to bring them back into the fold." That sounds a little softer than, "God manipulates people's choices." And it's a prayer that many Christian parents utter when asking God to bring a son or daughter back into the church. There is great comfort in the belief that God will restore every prodigal who accepted Jesus in their childhood.

I don't mean to dash any parent's hope that God will restore to faith every wandering son or daughter. However, that hope does not negate the questions before us: Does God manipulate our choices? Does He manipulate our love? *And* will our love for Him really be genuine if it has been manipulated beyond our ability to choose?

Biblical Warnings about Losing One's Salvation

If a person's salvation is eternally secure, why did John warn his people about believing lies that could turn them away from Christ? The reason for the warnings is this: **Bible writers**

knew that sincere believers could be deceived and led astray to destruction.

So let's look at more of these biblical warnings that indicate a believer can lose salvation:

> For in the case of those who have once been enlightened and have tasted of the Heavenly gift and have been partakers of the Holy Spirit, and having tasted of the good word of God and the powers of the age to come, and then have fallen away, it is impossible to renew them again to repentance, since they again crucify to themselves the Son of God, and put Him to open shame. Hebrews 6:4-6 (NASB)

This text clearly indicates two realities: 1) A person can fall away (be eternally lost) even after repentance and tasting the "heavenly gift" in Christ. We know that their conversion included repentance because the text says that they cannot "again" come to repentance. 2) These lost souls did at one time receive ("partakers of") the Holy Spirit. Clearly, at one time they *were* Spirit-filled believers.

As part the initial conversion, if the person had repented, tasted of the heavenly gift and received the Holy Spirit, I think we can reasonably suggest that he was "sincere." The significance of this text cannot be undermined: Nowhere does the author imply that they fell away because their confession in Christ was not sincere.

Instead, the author of Hebrews goes to some length to convince readers otherwise. He wants his warning to be taken seriously. To paraphrase: *I know it's hard to believe that a person who has tasted the good Word of God and has tasted of eternal life in Christ and has partaken of the Holy Spirit could be lost, BUT it CAN happen. So be on guard that this doesn't happen to you.*

Isn't Sincerity at the Altar Enough?

Because this obvious interpretation undermines the "impossible-to-be-lost" doctrine, some Evangelical writers suggest that the phrase "fallen away" does not mean that they lost their salvation. Here's such an attempt as noted on the website, *Come Reason Ministries:*[15]

> So, if the passage is addressing saved people, we must find out what is meant by "impossible to renew them again to repentance." Let's look at that word repentance.
>
> Notice that it does not say it is impossible to renew them again to salvation. In fact, the Greek word for "fallen away" is "parapipto" which can literally be translated "to stumble or fall along side". It is not "apostosia" from which we get the idea of apostasy or apostate. So, what kind of repentance do we mean, and what are we falling away from?
>
> The person is a believer... but his opportunity for witness and his ability to impact other people (not to mention the service he could render for Christ) will be forever lost. The repentance that the writer to Hebrews speaks of is a repentance from dead works.

That's a rather odd explanation. Should the text then read like this? "[I]t is impossible for them to repent from *dead works*, since they again crucify to themselves the Son of God, and put Him to open shame."

"Dead works"? What is that? If it means sinful acts we've done, then the Bible clearly teaches that we CAN confess

---

[15] http://www.comereason.org/bibl_cntr/con060.asp#ixzz2uk2jWkOd.

our wrong, turn and go another direction. But if "dead works" means good things we failed to do, then I think a loving God will accept our apology for wasted opportunities.

It's quite understandable that the author of this alternate explanation says that his answer is somewhat confusing, yet he still offers it as a small morsel of hope that the passage might possibly be interpreted in other than an obvious manner: a person *can* fall away from salvation.

But his weak suggestion that "fallen away" is only a temporary deviation from faith and not an apostasy that ends in destruction is not supported by other biblical passages. Notice how Jesus uses "fall away" as an implication of being eternally lost.

Luke 8:13: Jesus told the parable of the sower in which some of the seed landed on rocky ground. Those seed quickly sprang up but faded and died in the hot sun. His interpretation: "Those on the rocky ground are the ones who receive the word with joy when they hear it, but they have no root. They believe for a while, but in the time of testing they *fall away.*"

It would be fair to say that "received the word with joy" means that they were pretty excited and sincere, yet their roots (faith) didn't grow deep enough to withstand tribulations that came later in life. And "they fall away" quite simply means that they died spiritually and are eternally lost. Jesus gave no hint in this parable that those who "fall away" have a happy ending. The only seeds in this parable that had a happy ending are those which grew in fertile ground.

In other biblical passages this concept of "fall away" is used synonymously with being eternally lost:

In 2 Peter 3:17 Peter warns: "Therefore, dear friends, since you have been forewarned, be on your guard so that you may not be carried away by the error of the lawless and fall from your **secure position.**"

How interesting that Peter says that the believer could *"fall from your secure position."* How secure is a "secure position" if one can fall from it? Seems that Peter is reminding us that we *can* be sincere in Jesus, yet still be "carried away" or "fall" and be eternally lost.

John 15:5-6;16:1: In the following passage Jesus warns his disciples that although they are spiritually connected, believing and following Him that if they don't "remain" in Him that they will wither and their end would be fiery destruction. "I am the vine; you are the branches. If you **remain** in me and I in you, you will bear much fruit; apart from me you can do nothing. If you do not remain in me, you are like a branch that is **thrown away** and withers; such branches are picked up, thrown into the **fire and burned… All this I have told you so that you will not fall away.**"

I don't think anyone can mistake Jesus' warning that one who "falls away" will be "burned" as referring to the lost state of those who fall away from belief.

Revelation 22:19 (KJV): John the Revelator writes that a person can have his name written in the book of life, but it can be removed: "If any man shall take away from the words of this prophecy. **God shall take away his part out of the book of life,** and out of the holy city, and from the things which are written in this book."

Matthew 18:3: One day Jesus gave a brutally clear warning about deception. After saying that we must become like a child in order to enter the kingdom, He follows with this strong warning: "If your hand or your foot causes you to stumble, cut it off and throw it away. It is better for you to enter life maimed or crippled than to have two hands or two feet and be **thrown into eternal fire.**"

Clearly the thought of "stumbling" is directly equated with "eternal fire." Believers can and do stumble, sometimes falling away into eternal destruction. This is why Jesus, Paul, and John warn us to be watchful, because the Devil goes around like a roaring lion seeking ways to destroy God's children.

Let me also remind you that whatever your belief you must finally ask: What does my belief say about the character of God? Applied to the "security-of-salvation" belief we must ask: If a person sincerely accepts Jesus but later denies his faith, will God manipulate him into coming back to faith before he dies?

If so, what does that say about God's love? The Bible tells us that His love is always based upon granting us the freedom to choose: "Choose you this day whom ye will serve." Joshua 24:15 (KJV)

Thinking Deeply

Is your security wholly based on a nebulous feeling of "just knowing" you were sincere at your conversion?

How can you be assured that you aren't one of those "seeds in rocky soil" of which Jesus said initially flourishes in Christ through the Spirit but withers away because the roots didn't grow deep enough?

Or perhaps you are the branch that currently is connected to Jesus the Vine, yet someday will fall away and wither?

Please understand that my desire is not to discourage you or undermine your faith in Jesus. Quite the opposite! Together let's discover a more beautiful Biblical understanding of what it means to be saved.

God and His Son want to spend eternity with you. As the Bible teaches, Jesus loves you. This we *know!*

Imagination Station #3

In Scripture, heaven is also described as a place of building and planting: *"And they shall build houses, and inhabit them; and they shall plant vineyards, and eat the fruit of them."* Isaiah 65:21 (KVJ)

For hundreds of years the geographical location of Israel made it an attractive prey for raiding parties from the north and east. Whether Philistines, Midianites, Amalekites, or some other neighboring nation, during the harvest season enemies of Israel commonly raided, pillaged, and stole from the Israelites. In fact, Gideon—the guy who led 300 warriors armed with trumpets and torches against a sleeping Midian camp of thousands of soldiers—was found quietly and secretively threshing wheat in a winepress *"to keep it from the Midianites."*

In Judges 6:1-4 the Israelites' sad plight is described: *"The Israelites did evil in the eyes of the* Lord, *and for seven years he gave them into the hands of the Midianites. Because the power of Midian was so oppressive, the Israelites prepared shelters for themselves in mountain clefts, caves and strongholds. Whenever the Israelites planted their crops, the Midianites, Amalekites and other eastern peoples invaded the country. They camped on the land and ruined the crops all the way to Gaza and did not spare a living thing for Israel, neither sheep nor cattle nor donkeys."*

Every season raiders destroyed their homes and ravaged their crops. So to people living under such austere and painful circumstances, the promise of building one's own home and living in it and actually enjoying the produce from your vineyard and gardens sounded like heaven—literally!

Are you in constant danger of being victimized by home invasion, flood, tornado, foreclosure, sink hole, hurricane, war, or earthquake?

*For you, heaven will be **security**.*

Chapter 4:

Why Conversion Isn't Enough

"You and I are not saved because we have enduring faith. We are saved because at a moment in time we expressed faith in our Lord."
Dr. Charles Stanley, *Eternal Security*, p. 190.

I come from a religious upbringing where one needed to be converted *and* become "perfect" in order to be assured of salvation. It was a "conversion PLUS good works" endeavor. Problem was, one never knew *when* or *if* enough good works had been done to be considered perfect. And those few dear souls who did convince themselves that they were no longer sinners seemed (from my limited observation) a bit quirky and weird. Do you suppose they had never read 1 John 1:8: "If we say that we have no sin, we deceive ourselves, and the truth is not in us"?

The response many would give to this "conversion PLUS good works" philosophy is articulated by the Apostle Paul when he professed to the Philippian jailer, "Believe in the Lord Jesus Christ and you shall be saved." Period! Nothing more.

Coupled with this straight forward text is the narrative of the thief on the cross who expressed belief, and the next moment Jesus promised him a place in Paradise. So the question nags: Is salvation merely an expression of a momentary belief in Jesus—a moment of conviction and sincere confession of faith in Jesus—-and nothing more?

Bible scholars know that a doctrine must be built upon the comparison of multiple Scriptural references *and* with the question: "Is this concept in harmony with the loving character of God?" When we sweep together a multitude of texts which speak of salvation, we find many that clearly imply that one's sincere conversion confession of belief in Jesus must be followed by an ongoing willing submission to Holy Spirit's process of transforming our characters (used synonymously for "heart") into the likeness of Jesus *if* we expect to live with God forever.

Choices after Conversion DO Affect Salvation

In other words, a sincere confession of belief in Jesus does immediately change our standing before God from being strangers and foreigners outside His kingdom to now being adopted sons and daughters, heirs of the kingdom. But biblical writers are very clear that how we choose to walk *after* conversion does affect our "heirs of the kingdom" status.

Jesus illustrated this in a parable about the wandering evil spirit in Matthew 12:43-45:

> When an impure spirit comes out of a person, it goes through arid places seeking rest and does not find it. Then it says, "I will return to the house I left." When it arrives, it finds the house unoccupied, swept clean and put in order. Then it goes and takes with it seven other spirits more wicked than itself, and they go in and live there.

And the final condition of that person is worse than the first.

Jesus commanded an evil spirit to leave its victim when He sensed a desire within that tortured mortal's heart to be free. Jesus never cast an evil spirit out of the heart of a person who enjoyed being possessed. We might think of this deliverance as a type of conversion where the heart calls out to God for help and divine power responds. But, as this parable warns, deliverance from an evil spirit must be followed by a filling of a different spirit, i.e, the Holy Spirit. If not, then a person can regress again into a sinful life that is seven times worse than before experiencing Jesus' power in his life.

"Well," someone may quip, "that just shows that his conversion wasn't really sincere." Not true. The desire for deliverance was sincere and God sincerely cast out the evil spirit. The parable doesn't question the sincerity or reality of the initial deliverance. Rather, it focuses on what that person does AFTER his deliverance. If he doesn't fill his heart (house) with God's spirit (which we might call "walking in the Spirit"), then his life becomes seven times worse. In other words, he is not only tormented in this life but also forfeits heaven.

At this point you may think that I'm slipping back into a "salvation by faith PLUS good deeds" philosophy. Not true. The "good deeds" philosophy will always haunt a person: Have I done enough? Have I confessed all of my sins? Have I done enough to warrant forgiveness and eternal life? Have I lived a good enough life in recent years to outweigh my earlier life of sin? Is there something I have unknowingly failed to do? Am I guilty of the sin of omission? Do I have *enough* faith?

The WhatEVER-Factor person doesn't see God as a bookkeeper who is always checking to see if he has been nice enough to offset his naughtiness. Rather, God is a loving Father—longing to find children who really WANT to live with

Him forever and are showing such by their growing desire and enjoyment of walking with Him in the Spirit. *Here and now.*

God is not looking for people who have achieved enough to be saved. He is looking for folks who, like Paul, "want to do good... for in my inner being I delight in God's law." Romans 7:21

Saving Those Who Will ENJOY Living with Him... Forever

Beings of like minds and like spirits enjoy each other's company. As such, *God will save those who will ENJOY living with Him forever because their hearts and minds are being changed right now into His likeness.*

Pause and think about that. Common sense alone tells us that Jesus will only take people to heaven who will *enjoy* being with Him forever. If someone confesses faith in Jesus but doesn't enjoy His fellowship now, why take him to heaven to forever be immersed in that fellowship? If that person doesn't find pleasure in walking with Jesus now in an obedient relationship, imagine how unpleasant heaven would be. Would that person need regular "vacations" from heaven to let his hair down and raise some *hell*?

This reminds me of my "Dear Judy" phone call from yesteryear. I was a freshman in high school. One day Judy (not her real name) caught my notice, and the attraction was mutual. We dated steadily for several months. Judy was a really nice girl and easy on the eye. But I was young and my heart began to drift.

The steady relationship, for a time so exhilarating, began to feel stifling and restrictive. Finally one evening I cranked up my courage and phoned her. After beating around the bush for a while, I finally got to the point. "Judy, I want to just be your friend, not your boyfriend."

Judy, in later years, told my mom that she was crushed by the call. But to this day my mom reminds me that when I hung up the phone I went running and jumping through the house, shouting, "I'm FREE! Whoopee, I'm free!"

Will there be people like that in heaven? They think Jesus is pretty nice, but feel stifled by constantly living according to His will. Because they had a "come to Jesus moment," they were taken to heaven. Will they need regular Sabbaticals from heaven—to escape its stifling atmosphere? Maybe we'll hear them singing as they temporarily disappear beyond the blue: "I'm FREE! Whoopee, I'm finally free!"

Let's review some more texts that demonstrate the importance of character transformation in those who will enjoy heaven.

Matthew 18:3 (KJV): "*Except ye be converted, and become as little children, ye shall not enter into the kingdom of heaven.*" Notice that Jesus didn't say, "Be sincerely converted and you shall enter the kingdom." Rather, *be converted AND become as little children.*

Jesus' command to become as little children easily negates the old notion that one must become perfect through good deeds and disciplined living. Those attributes are not commonly attributed to children. So, what childlike attributes was Jesus wanting us to emulate?

Some have suggested self-forgetfulness, simplicity, or confiding love. The phrase "childlike trust" often comes to mind. Whatever your definition of "like a child," the important thing is that we must "become" something *subsequent* to being converted.

After saying that we must become like a child in order to enter the kingdom, Jesus followed with this strong warning in verse 8: "If your hand or your foot causes you to stumble, cut it off and throw it away. It is better for you to enter life maimed or crippled than to have two hands or two feet and be thrown into eternal fire."

The logical question is, "Stumble from what?" Logical answer: To stumble or fall on our walk from conversion to eternity. This statement adds a serious dose of importance to the childlike character change that Jesus says the redeemed must experience.

Interesting that Jesus did not say: "Cut off your hand if it is causes you to stumble, for the sin that you stumble into and willingly continue will NOT keep you from the kingdom (being eternally secured at your conversion). Nevertheless you will enjoy heaven more if you overcome." No, it was not an "enjoy heaven more" nor be a "better witness" nor "bring glory to God" context. It was a "kingdom versus everlastingly lost" context. Thus, without character change, your conversion alone will NOT be enough.

In Matthew 7:22-27 (KJV) we find a most troubling saying of Jesus:

> Not every one who saith unto me, "Lord, Lord," shall enter into the kingdom of heaven; but he that doeth the will of my Father which is in heaven. Many will say to me in that day, "Lord, Lord, have we not prophesied in thy name? and in thy name have cast out devils? and in thy name done many wonderful works?"
>
> And then will I profess unto them, "I never knew you: depart from me, ye that work iniquity.'"

Now notice how Jesus follows with an emphasis upon doing what He teaches. A mere profession of faith (or we might say a mere citing of "I am saved because I accepted Jesus as my Lord and Savior") is not enough. It must be followed by a certain *becoming*. A reference, again, to the necessity of a character change. If that is not happening in a Christian's life, then Jesus

says that such a person's claim on eternal life is as secure as building one's house on a sandy foundation.
Read on. Vs 24-27:

> Therefore whosoever heareth these sayings of mine, and doeth them, I will liken him unto a wise man, which built his house upon a rock: and the rain descended, and the floods came, and the winds blew, and beat upon that house; and it fell not: for it was founded upon a rock.
>
> And every one that heareth these sayings of mine, and doeth them not, shall be likened unto a foolish man, which built his house upon the sand: and the rain descended, and the floods came, and the winds blew, and beat upon that house; and it fell: and great was the fall of it.

Notice in the text that Jesus equates "knowing Jesus" with "doing what I have commanded." He clearly states that both are necessary if a person is to live with Him forever. To think otherwise, He says, is like building your hope of eternal life on eroding sand.

This "knowing and doing" combination is reiterated by John who applies the "doing what Jesus commands" with loving one's brother. 1 John 2:4-6, 9-12 (KJV):

> And hereby we do KNOW that we know him, if we keep his commandments. He that saith, 'I know him,' and keepeth not his commandments, is a liar, and the TRUTH IS NOT IN HIM. But whoso keepeth his word, in him verily is the love of God perfected: hereby know we that we are in him. He that saith he abideth in him ought himself also so to WALK, EVEN AS HE WALKED.

He that saith he is in the light, and hateth his brother, is in darkness even until now. He that loveth his brother abideth in the light, and there is none occasion of stumbling in him. But he that hateth his brother is in darkness, and walketh in darkness, and knoweth not whither he goeth, because that darkness hath blinded his eyes. write unto you, little children, because your sins are forgiven you for his name's sake.

Notice that John is writing to converted believers who know that their sins are forgiven but are not walking in the light of Jesus' love. They are walking in darkness.

Light versus Darkness

What does "walking in the darkness" mean? Jesus' kingdom is light; Satan's kingdom is darkness. The Bible is clear:
- Light enshrouded the pillar of cloud by day and the pillar of fire by night, leading the Israelites through the wilderness. Exodus 13:21
- Light filled the tabernacle of Moses when God's presence was manifest. Exodus 24:17
- Light shone from Moses' face after spending time with God on Mt. Sinai. Exodus 34:29
- Light filled the temple of Solomon at its dedication. 2 Chronicles 7
- Light shone on the hills of Bethlehem when the angels announced Jesus' birth. Luke 2:14
- Jesus said, "I am the light of the world." John 8:12
- In the beginning Jesus caused the "light to shine out of darkness." 2 Corinthians 4:6 (KJV)
- Jesus is the "true light, which lighteth every man that cometh into the world." John 1:9 (KJV)

- He that followeth Me, "Jesus said, "shall not walk in darkness, but shall have the light of life." John 8:12 (KJV)

Darkness is the opposite of God and His kingdom and symbolizes Satan's realm:
- 1 Samuel 2:9: "He will guard the feet of his faithful servants, but the wicked will be silenced in the place of darkness."
- Proverbs 4:19: "But the way of the wicked is like deep darkness."
- 1 John 1:5: "God is light; in him there is no darkness at all."
- 1 John 1:6: "If we claim to have fellowship with him and yet walk in the darkness, we lie and do not live out the truth."
- Matthew 8:12: "But the children of the kingdom shall be cast out into outer darkness: there shall be weeping and gnashing of teeth." (Notice these are "children of the kingdom" who are cast into outer darkness which means they at one time were "adopted" into God's family through conversion.)
- Matthew 22:13 (KJV): "Then said the king to the servants, 'Bind him hand and foot, and take him away, and cast him into outer darkness.'"
- John 8:12 (KJV): "Then spake Jesus again unto them, saying, 'I am the light of the world: he that followeth me shall not walk in darkness, but shall have the light of life.'"
- Ephesians 5:8 (KJV): "For ye were sometimes darkness, but now are ye light in the Lord: walk as children of light."
- Colossians 1:13 (KJV): "Who hath delivered us from the power of darkness, and hath translated us into the kingdom of his dear Son." (Compare this with Matt.

8:12 where Jesus says that a "child of the kingdom" can, by his choices and attitude be cast out of the kingdom. Thus, Jesus contradicts those who say, "After being adopted into God's family, we will not be kicked out."

With this understanding that darkness is associated with Satan, hell, damnation, and lostness, it's of consequence that John 2:3 says the evidence of "knowing Jesus" (or evidence that we are "children of light" on our way to the kingdom) is not merely sincerity but a willingness to "walk as Jesus walked" in love.

Please note that John clarifies in verse 12 that he's writing to folks who *know* that their sins are forgiven. Thus he's speaking to "converted" Christians who have accepted Jesus forgiveness on the cross.[16] Yet, John says they are still in "darkness" if they still hate their brother. Darkness is synonymous with Satan, sin and death. No person who harbors a "dark" attitude toward another will be in heaven.

Jesus said, "And this is the condemnation, that light is come into the world, and men loved darkness rather than light, because their deeds were evil." John 3:19 (KJV)

Hatred is darkness; darkness is evil. There shall be no evil thing in heaven: as such, heaven is for those whose attitudes are being transformed from darkness to light, from hatred to love.

Therefore, a character change is necessary because (and this is simple logic) there will be no brother haters in heaven. As it should be! What would heaven be if its residents hate their neighbors? Does being translated to heaven instantaneously change us from brother haters to brother lovers? Of course

---

[16] In reality Jesus' death on the cross extended forgiveness to every person. We don't need to beg for forgiveness if God already made it available. The challenge is whether we will accept His forgiveness AND allow that forgiveness to instill in us a whatEVER attitude toward becoming transformed into His likeness.

not. That is a character transformation that must be in process on earth.

A revivalist was preaching this message of brotherly love and noting how important it is for each to search their hearts and seek forgiveness and peace. "Is there any one here tonight who can honestly say that there isn't one living person to whom you harbor a feeling of bitterness or hatred... be it a parent, former spouse, neighbor or church member? If there is such a person, will you please stand?"

Not expecting any honest person to stand, the preacher was surprised when in the back of the congregation Brother Hawkins stood up. He was a scowly old fellow who had few kind words and his faced showed such.

"My brother, are you saying that there is not another living soul that you have no bitterness or hated toward?" asked the surprised revivalist.

"That's right, sir."

"Please tell us the secret to your victory."

"Them scoundrels all up and died on me."

Salvation does not come by old age wherein our characters are miraculously transformed because our contrary relationships die off. Transformation comes when the Spirit of God is allowed to come into our heart and help us choose love over hate... where *"old things pass away and all things become new."* 1 Corinthians 5:17

Now *that's* the secret to victory!

But if Brother Hawkins wants to be heaven-bound, does he *need* to experience an attitude change even if as a child he in all sincerity walked to the altar and accepted Jesus? Does that childhood event guarantee his salvation regardless of his bitter character? According to my Bible, unrepentant scoundrels won't be in heaven. They just wouldn't be happy there.

Imagination Station #4

"When the Son of Man sits on his glorious throne, you who have followed me will also sit on twelve thrones, judging the twelve tribes of Israel. And everyone who has left houses or brothers or sisters or father or mother or wife or children or fields for my sake will receive a hundred times as much and will inherit eternal life." Matthew 19:28-29

By Jesus' day the Israelites had suffered under the harsh yoke of the dictatorial Romans for generations. To sit on a throne and rule with freedom and honor was only a vapor of a wish. Jesus now offers them a place of honor.

Don't we all wish to be respected and honored? So, in heaven will we actually sit on thrones of judgment? Honor and respect comes in many forms. Which form might be the most enticing for you? (I'll discuss this subject in more detail in Section III.)

The best answer is the honor of enjoying a personal fellowship with Jesus that will only deepen and become more fulfilling throughout eternity. Just as a good marriage grows through seasons of learning, knowing, and doing "life" together, an eternity with Jesus will have similar seasons of growing and fulfillment. Think of this as love and joy on heavenly steroids!

We love to share experiences with our loved ones. And often it's the togetherness that enhances the whole activity, whether we're gourmet or picnic eating, exploring, thrill seeking, or soaking up the awesome view of sunsets, ocean, mountains, and fall colors.

Eternal community with Jesus: that would be **heaven.**

Chapter 5:

Salvation Is Not a Birthright

"If you were Abraham's children, you would be doing what Abraham did." Jesus

The Pharisees believed heaven was guaranteed by their birthright.

The Evangelical's belief that their salvation is eternally secure after conversion has its counterpart in the Pharisee's mistaken understanding that the promises made by God to their Father Abraham were irreversibly guaranteed to the children of Abraham... especially to the Pharisaical leaders of Israel. Both groups believe that a son can never be cast out of the family and disinherited. The Pharisees were sons by birth because they were sons of Abraham and, thus, part of the divine family. The Christian is an "adopted" son or daughter in God's family by rebirth, i.e. conversion and baptism.

This Evangelical notion is clearly implied in statements such as these:

- "After being adopted into God's family (Romans 8:15), we will not be kicked out." www*GotQuestion.org*.

- "Even if a believer for all practical purposes becomes an unbeliever, his salvation is not in jeopardy." Dr. Charles Stanley, *Eternal Security*, p. 93.
- "Christ will not deny an unbelieving Christian his or her salvation because to do so would be to deny Himself." Dr. Charles Stanley, *Eternal Security*, p. 94.

In a similar manner, the Pharisees claimed to possess an irreversible heavenly inheritance, as seen by Jesus' narrative in John 8:37-47 (RSV):

> I know that you are Abraham's descendants. Yet you are trying to kill me because you've not received what I've told you. I declare what I've seen in my Father's presence, and you're doing what you've heard from your father.
>
> They replied to him, "Our father is Abraham!"
>
> Jesus told them, "If you were Abraham's children, you would be doing what Abraham did. But now you're trying to kill me, a man who has told you the truth that I heard from God. Abraham wouldn't have done that. You are doing your father's actions."
>
> They told him, "We're not illegitimate children. We have one Father, God himself."
>
> Jesus told them, "If God were your Father, you would've loved me, because I came from God and am here. I haven't come on my own accord, but he sent me. Why don't you understand what I've said? It's because you can't listen to my words. You belong to your father the Devil, and

you want to carry out the desires of your father. He was a murderer from the beginning and has never stood for truth, since there is no truth in him. Whenever he tells a lie, he speaks in character, because he is a liar and the father of lies. But it is because I speak the truth that you don't believe me. Can any of you prove me guilty of sin? If I'm telling the truth, why don't you believe me? The one who belongs to God listens to the words of God. The reason you don't listen is because you don't belong to God.'"

The Pharisees were the descendants (children) of Abraham. Thus, they were genetically correct in saying that they were "children of Abraham." There are many texts where God assures the children of Abraham that they were His family and, therefore, recipients of His eternal blessings. But in this dialogue the Pharisees are offended because Jesus is saying that they aren't the *real* children of Abraham, NOT part of God's blessed family and NOT in line to receive God's promised blessings.

Jesus told them that their claim to eternal inheritance could be established not merely by their genealogy but by doing the works of Abraham—having the character and faith of Abraham. The true children of Abraham would live as he lived, following a life of obedience to God. They would not try to kill Jesus who was speaking the truth given Him from God.

In plotting against Christ, the rabbis were not doing the works of Abraham. A mere lineal descent from Abraham was of no eternal value. Quoting Old Testament texts where God made many promises to Israel was not enough. Without a spiritual connection with Him, as manifested in possessing the same spirit and doing the same works as Jesus, they were not God's children.

Jesus denied that the Jewish leaders were children of Abraham. He said, "You do the deeds of your father. If God were your Father, you would love Me; for I proceeded forth and came from God." Clearly, their works, not their lineage, revealed their real father as seen here: "You are of your father the devil and the lusts of your father it is your will to do." Vs. 44-45

Guaranteed Salvation Is Likeness of Character

Jesus' underlying challenge was apostolic succession. Their claim to salvation because they were children of Abraham was to be proven—not by name and lineage—but by likeness of character. A life actuated by the spirit of Abraham (and in our case by the Spirit of Christ) is the evidence of who our true Father is. Thus, our works (character revealed in our thoughts and actions), not merely a profession that we have been adopted into God's family through our sincere conversion, reveals our real Father.

With Jesus' words as a backdrop of truth, let's rethink Dr. Stanley's statement: "Christ will not deny an unbelieving Christian his or her salvation because to do so would be to deny Himself."

Stanley suggests that a person who becomes a reborn child of God at conversion can never be lost. Why? Because God will never disown a member of His family. But isn't that actually the opposite of biblical truth? Jesus said Pharisees who have the character of Satan are not God's children. God only grants His blessings to His children.

So, when children of Abraham act like the Devil they are cutting themselves off from the family of God, thus forfeiting God's promised blessings. In fact, for God to grant His blessings to these devilish Pharisees would mean that God would be denying Himself. He would be contradicting His own words that His blessings are only for His children.

Compare the words of both Paul and Jesus. Paul reminds us that we were once children of Satan but through Jesus we become children of God: "For ye were sometimes darkness, but now are ye light in the Lord: walk as children of light." Ephesians 5:8 (KJV)

Jesus reminded the Jews that a child of light CAN end up being cast out into darkness: "But the children of the kingdom shall be cast out into outer darkness: there shall be weeping and gnashing of teeth." Matthew 8:12 (KJV)[17]

Paul tells the Philippians that he has a goal for himself: to be transformed so that he has the mind of Christ. He hasn't reached that goal, but is determined to "press on" walking in the Spirit:

> I want to know Christ—yes, to know the power of his resurrection and participation in his sufferings, becoming like him in his death, and so, somehow, attaining to the resurrection from the dead. Not that I have already obtained all this, or have already arrived at my goal, but I press on to take hold of that for which Christ Jesus took hold of me. Brothers and sisters, I do not consider myself yet to have taken hold of it. But one thing I do: Forgetting what is behind and straining toward what is ahead, I press on toward the goal to win the prize for which God has called me heavenward in Christ Jesus." Philippians 3:10-14

Even at the end of his life, Paul doesn't say he has achieved all that he told the Philippians he was striving to obtain. But his

---

[17] Dr. Charles Stanley offers a mind bending answer to this dilemma. He suggests that "caste into outer darkness where there will be weeping and gnashing of teeth" is not a state of lostness. It's merely an area of heaven which is less desirable. We'll analyze this in the chapter. "Holy Living Earns Heavenly Rewards."

assurance of salvation is stronger than ever. Why? Not because he achieved, but because he did not give up on faith.

If You're Still Running the Race...

Metaphors are helpful, but we must always understand their limitations. In this "running the race" analogy do not think that Paul won the salvation crown because he had accomplished something great. One might mistakenly read that into the phrase, "I have finished the course." He wasn't saying that he had done all that he desired for the kingdom nor that he had become fully transformed into the likeness of Christ. His course (or life) had come to an end. But he had never stopped fighting the darkness. He had kept the faith, running still toward the light.

I guess we could say that nothing Satan had thrown at him had caused Paul to quit the race. Paul's WhatEVER Factor had not changed. Late in life Paul writes to Timothy and expresses his assurance that heaven is in his future:

> For I am now ready to be offered, and the time of my departure is at hand. I have fought a good fight, I have finished my course, I have kept the faith: Henceforth there is laid up for me a crown of righteousness, which the Lord, the righteous judge, shall give me at that day: and not to me only, but unto all them also that love his appearing. 2 Timothy 4:6-8 (KJV)

How did Paul know that a crown awaited him? Was it because of his Damascus Road conversion? That dramatic experience was an absolutely sincere and sobering conversion. Yes, that was the start, but Paul doesn't even mention that in his farewell. Instead, he says he's heaven-bound because he didn't give up! No matter the challenges, he kept fighting to hold on to his faith in the Lord. He kept walking in the Spirit on the pathway to heaven despite many disappointments and failures. He doesn't say he is perfect nor worthy, rather he just kept running towards the light.

When he stumbles (as referenced in Romans Chapter 7: "I do that which I don't want to do"), he gets up and keeps running. He doesn't turn his back on the light and fall back into darkness.

Can you see how irrelevant Paul's conversation with Timothy would be if all he needed to say is: "I am about to die but I know I will have eternal life because I had a Damascus road conversion. Period! *Oh, yes, I'm glad I didn't stumble and lose my faith but my crown was never in question.*" If that were all that was important then why would Paul go on to say that he KNEW a crown awaited him BECAUSE he didn't give up the race.

His walking mantra was, "WhatEVER I eat or drink or whatEVER I do, I want to do for the glory of God."

The writer of Hebrews also uses the same metaphor: walking in the Spirit akin to running a race. Generally, we think of rewards given to the runner who *finishes* the race ahead of others. But in this metaphor Paul implies that all who are saved have finished the race successfully.

> Hebrews 12:1-3: "Therefore, since we are surrounded by such a great cloud of witnesses, let us throw off everything that hinders and the sin that so easily entangles. And let us run with perseverance the race marked out for us, fixing our eyes on Jesus, the pioneer and perfecter of faith. For the joy that was set before him he endured the cross, scorning its shame, and sat down at the right hand of the throne of God. Consider him who endured such opposition from sinners, so that you will not grow weary and lose heart."

Eternal Life *Is* Knowing Jesus

John 17: 3: "Now this is eternal life, that they may know you, the only true God, and Jesus Christ, whom you have sent."

This may sound like mere head knowledge, but the biblical "know" most often refers to an intimate, personal, interactive relationship. In fact, the Bible often refers to the sexual relationship between a wife and husband as "they knew one another" and the wife became pregnant. As such, it is helpful to interchange the word "know" with "love." Thus John 17:3 could read: "This is eternal life that they may love you, the only real God, and Jesus the anointed, whom you have sent." Bottom line, we can't love someone we don't know; and to really know God is to love him. Will you receive eternal life if you confess faith in Jesus, yet you don't "know" or love Him?

John 14:6-9: "Jesus answered, 'I am the way and the truth and the life. No one comes to the Father except through me. If you really know me, you will know my Father as well. From now on, you do know him and have seen him... Anyone who has seen me has seen the Father.'"

I come from a tradition that enjoyed saying, "We have the truth." While well-intentioned, that never felt completely comfortable to me. Now I think I'm discovering why. Salvation is to KNOW the truth which means to know and love Jesus. No one HAS the truth nor HAS salvation, since that sounds more like a piece of knowledge or some other possession. (Remember my "Bar Code Salvation" illustration in the Introduction?) We may know OF Jesus and what He taught but eternal life is based upon KNOWING Jesus in a love relationship. Does knowing and loving Jesus make a noticeable change in our attitudes and behavior?

Here's another great text. John 14:23-24: "Anyone who loves me will obey my teaching. My Father will love them, and we will come to them and make our home with them. Anyone who does not love me will not obey my teaching. These words you hear are not my own; they belong to the Father who sent me."

Yes, if we know/love Jesus we will start living as Jesus lived. Jesus compares this concept with freedom and slavery in John 8:31-38. So Jesus was saying to those Jews who had believed Him:

> "If you continue in My word, then you are truly disciples of Mine; and you will know the truth, and the truth will make you free." They answered Him, "We are Abraham's descendants and have never yet been enslaved to anyone; how is it that you say, 'You will become free?'"
>
> Jesus answered them, "Truly, truly, I say to you, everyone who commits sin is the slave of sin. The slave does not remain in the house forever; the son does remain forever. So if the Son makes you free, you will be free indeed. My word has no place in you. I speak the things which I have seen with My Father; therefore you also do the things which you heard from your father.'"

So, when we sin in attitude or behavior, it shows that we are slaves to sin and Satan, at least in that area of our life. When Jesus, through His Spirit, is invited by us to move into that room or area of our life, then He unshackles us from that sin and kicks the Devil out. Evidence of change is seen in a change in our character.

No Citizen of Heaven Will Be a Slave to Satan

Jesus did say that we cannot be slaves to two masters. Either God or Satan is in control of areas of our life. The apostle John later writes about this dichotomy:

> Dear friends, let us love one another, for love comes from God. Everyone who loves has been born of God and knows God. Whoever does not love does not know God, because God is love... Whoever lives in love lives in God, and God in them. This is how love is made complete among us so that we will have confidence on the day of judgment: In this world we are like Jesus... (Example:) If we say we love God yet hate a brother or sister, we are liars. For if we do not love a fellow believer, whom we have seen, we cannot love God, whom we have not seen." 1 John 4:7-8, 16-17

So, if we know and love God, we have been set free from gossip, but if we still love to gossip it shows we don't know/love God and are still slaves of Satan in that area.

- If we know/love God, we are free from lying and dishonesty, but if we continually practice dishonesty, that shows we are slaves still.
- If we know/love God, we are free from destructive anger and desire to get even.
- If we know/love God, we are free from the enslavement to sex that drives us to live immoral lives.
- If we know/love God, we are free from selfish greed.

Does that sound like salvation by right living? It might unless we understand the basic intention. If we have a WHATever attitude toward our sin, meaning that we think it's no big deal and God isn't hung up on our behavior and will forgive it (in other words, if we are making excuse for our sin), then we don't know/love God and his grace does not cover our sin.

However, if our passion is like that of Paul's when he said "WhatEVER I eat or drink or whatEVER I do I want to do for the glory of God" then the whole picture changes.

Salvation Is Not a Birthright

This means that Paul was passionately seeking to know, love, and live the life of Jesus. BUT he's still a sinful being and he stumbles along the way. A stumble is different than choosing to sin and making excuse. When Paul stumbled, he HATED it. In Romans 7 he writes, "Some things I don't want to do, I do. I hate that. I'm still enslaved to that sin in my life. Who is able to deliver me? Thanks to be God through Jesus Christ I have the victory."

There is no question where Paul's mind is. He has a mind for Christ, but still stumbles. That's much different than having a knowledge of God and His will, but choosing to practice sin AND make excuse for it.

Now, was Paul condemned when he stumbled? No, in Romans 8 he says that we who have that passion to be transformed into the likeness of Jesus are NOT under condemnation when we stumble. Like the woman caught in adultery, Jesus says to us, "I do not condemn you. Now go and sin no more." In other words, claiming the victory over that sin in your life by knowing and loving me!

So we CAN stumble and not be condemned, AND we can do righteous deeds yet be condemned: Jesus gave an example showing that even if we appear to be righteous He knows if our motivation is based upon selfish desire for appearance and power or the result of knowing and loving Jesus.

> Luke 13:22-27: Then Jesus went through the towns and villages, teaching as he made his way to Jerusalem. Someone asked him, "Lord, are only a few people going to be saved?"
>
> He said to them, 'Make every effort to enter through the narrow door, because many, I tell you, will try to enter and will not be able to. Once the owner of the house gets up and closes

the door, you will stand outside knocking and pleading, 'Sir, open the door for us."

But he will answer, 'I don't know you or where you come from."

Then you will say, 'We ate and drank with you, and you taught in our streets.'

But he will reply, "I don't know you or where you come from. Away from me, all you evildoers!'"

This means that when we stand at the gates of heaven, we don't gain entrance merely because we have a bar code that reads: "On January 3, 2009, I accepted Jesus and I was really sincere" nor because we think we have the truth nor because of the plethora of righteous deeds. Nor does it mean that we have to be perfect to enter, because we are still a work in progress.

The issue is "Is my heart's desire to know/love Jesus? If it is, then my passion will be to have the character of Jesus and live like Him in every area of life... a whatEVER attitude. Or am I continuing to choose to be enslaved to Satan and His will with a WHATever attitude in any area of my life?"

No one will enter heaven who has the attitude: "I seek freedom from sin in this area, but this other area is no big deal." We cannot enter heaven while still choosing to be enslaved to two masters.

How do I know if I love Jesus enough? It's not a matter of how much. It's a matter of our heart's passion: Are you seeking to know/love Jesus? When you do, He will reveal sin in your life. When he reveals sin, are you crying out for God to free you? Or do you choose to remain enslaved to Satan's sin? Remember eternity with God is about a relationship— not bookkeeping. And a loving relationship with God elicits sincere repentance when we recognize that we are broken and stumbling sinners.

But a question might remain: "I agree with what your saying, but some sins are *small* sins and God must think differently about them. The Catholics call these little sins *venial* which means "a relatively slight sin that that does not entail damnation of the soul."

Does God grade sins as we do, i.e. small vs. big; venial vs. mortal? Let's look at that in the next chapter.

Imagination Station #5

*So heaven is a special place of **relief, security** and **togetherness** with Jesus.*

*To a high school student, who seldom worries about death and whose greatest pain may be failing to attract that cool guy or drop-dead beautiful girl, heaven's promise of **relief, security** and Divine **relationship** may hardly wiggle the needle on their excitement meter.*

To most teenagers "riding on a lion" is a heavenly motivation that probably could be surpassed by an experience on earth. To Johnny nothing he had heard about heaven surpassed his anticipation of chocolate cake for dinner.

Many have a similar hesitation: "I believe in heaven but it sounds really boring, and there are some things I want to enjoy before Jesus returns… and puts an end to my fun!"

Often their picture of heaven is where you're expected to wear a long white robe, listen to harp music, walk around the park, and recite Bible verses. Confined to a monastery might be the picture that comes to mind. A place where you can't roll in the mud, go swimming, run too fast or laugh too hard. A place of peace and quiet.

One author wrote: "What would be a more terrible fate for the righteous than to spend unnumbered eons in enforced idleness? Could the wicked suffer a fate worse than this supposed weightless semi-transparent existence with no chance to shut off the everlasting harp music?"

Let me try to stretch your imagination—which, in my opinion, is not that different from your stomach. If we continually eat small amounts, then our stomach shrinks and so do our cravings. Likewise, if we don't stretch our imagination about heaven, then our vision narrows and fades simply to no pain, no hassles, building a house, gardening, sitting on a throne… and riding a lion. Or eating chocolate cake. EVERY DAY.

Chapter 6:

Would You Marry a Nymphomaniac?

✝

Nymphomania [nim'fəmā'nē·ə]: Etymology: Gk, nymphe, maiden, mania, madness. "Psychosexual disorder of women characterized by an insatiable desire for sexual satisfaction."

Decades ago, when I was younger and more naïve, I saw a bumper sticker on the little VW of the college girl next door: "Warning, I am a nymphomaniac!"

I wasn't sure what that big word meant. Was it some kind of water creature—like a water maiden or mermaid? But I had a slight suspicion that it was more sinister. Maybe even kind of naughty.

Now with much of life behind me and still enjoying forty-seven years with a committed and loving wife, I ask myself— and I ask you: Would you marry a nymphomaniac, someone whose insatiable desire for sexual satisfaction could never be satisfied by just one partner?

As a pastor who has officiated at more weddings than I can remember, I can just imagine standing at the marriage altar and asking the nymphomaniac bride, "Do you take this man to be your wedded husband and promise to keep yourself only unto him as long as you both shall live?"

"I'll do my best, but no promises," she might reply. Or "Maybe... WHATever."

You're Married to Jesus

May I suggest that the kind of people who go to heaven will *not* be there because they were perfectly obedient and kept all the rules. Nor because, like the servant with ten talents, they have worked harder than others. Nor because they gave more money to the church, nor healed more people, nor prayed greater prayers, nor led larger churches, nor had the greater natural gifts.

The primary virtue of the saved will be that they love God with all their hearts and love their neighbors as themselves. In other words, they are there because of their character. It has been transformed (or more realistically, was being transformed) to reflect the loving character of Jesus. SO, heaven is for people who relate to God and one another in a manner described by Fruit of the Spirit.[18]

The Bible uses the metaphor of marriage for conversion and commitment to Jesus Christ. He becomes your bridegroom and you, His bride. This marriage metaphor is referenced often in Scripture[19]:

In the Old Testament the nation of Israel was called God's wife. Too often she was an adulterous wife—a nymphomaniac, if you will.

---

[18] Galatians 5:22-24 – "The fruit of the Spirit is love, joy, peace, forbearance, kindness, goodness, faithfulness, gentleness self-control. Against such things there is no law. Those who belong to Christ Jesus have crucified the flesh with its passions and desires."

[19] We'll explore in greater depth the biblical metaphor of Israel and/or the church being Jesus' wife in Section VI.

From Ezekiel 16:32-34: "You adulterous wife! You prefer strangers to your own husband! All prostitutes receive gifts, but you give gifts to all your lovers, bribing them to come to you from everywhere for your illicit favors."

In the New Testament the Apostle Paul refers to the Corinthian church as God's bride: "I am jealous for you with a godly jealousy. I promised you to one husband, to Christ, so that I might present you as a pure virgin to him." 2 Corinthians 11:2

Often I have reminded folks that their verbal commitment to accept Jesus as Lord and Savior is their spiritual engagement commitment and their baptism is a public ritual and demonstration of their new relationship, similar to a wedding ceremony. At your baptism you are confessing your vow verbally: "I have accepted Jesus and promise to live for Him till death." And to the witnesses of your baptism you are saying: "Celebrate my new state of spiritual oneness with Jesus and, because you love me, help me to be true to my vow."

God intends for each party to make it a whatEVER commitment. God did whatEVER it took to open the door to salvation by Jesus' death on the cross. He expects you, His bride, to make a similar "whatever-it-takes" commitment in return. Note these texts:

> He who loves father or mother more than Me is not worthy of Me. And he who loves son or daughter more than Me is not worthy of Me. And he who does not take his cross and follow after Me is not worthy of Me. Matthew 10:37-38 (NKJV)

> No one can serve two masters. Either you will hate the one and love the other, or you will be devoted to the one and despise the other. You cannot serve both God and money." Matthew 6:24

Don't you know that when you offer yourselves to someone as obedient slaves, you are slaves of the one you obey—whether you are slaves to sin, which leads to death, or to obedience, which leads to righteousness? But thanks be to God that, though you used to be slaves to sin, you have come to obey from your heart the pattern of teaching that has now claimed your allegiance. You have been set free from sin and have become slaves to righteousness.
Romans 6:16-18

Any Sin Is Adultery

In our earthly marriages, we have observed varying levels of commitment among partners and even varying levels of commitment toward different issues within each marriage. In some areas of marriage we may have a WHATever attitude; in other areas, a whatEVER commitment.

For example, several years ago a lay leader of my church bought a motorcycle without consulting his wife. Worse still, he tried to hide his purchase from her by storing it at his business warehouse. But wives have an intuitive sense of knowing.

Her opposition to him owning a motorcycle was firmly based. As a registered nurse, she had seen too many mangled bodies scraped off the pavement. Often these were men who were riding in a safe manner but were wiped out by a motorist who didn't look twice.

"Hey, I got a great deal on a motorcycle, but my wife doesn't have a clue." He was a bit of a braggart as well.

"But she will. What then?" I warned.

"Oh, she'll get all upset and won't talk to me for a couple weeks. But she'll eventually get over it. She won"t like it and won't ride with me, but she'll eventually stop fussing."

This WHATever attitude he had toward his wife on this issue can be restated: "Ah, she won't like it, but it's no big deal. She won't divorce me!"

Now, if this same fellow were to spend a weekend with another woman in a secret hideaway, his marriage would be OVER! So in THAT area of his marriage he knows to maintain a whatEVER attitude, i.e., "WhatEVER I do against her wishes, I will *not* do that!"

Most marriages are a mix of WHATever and whatEVER. Some things are considered minor offenses while others are marriage killers. Sometimes there *must* be a WHATever attitude in some areas of marriage, because neither we nor our spouse consistently make reasonable demands—at least in our own opinion.

Problem: Most of us carry this mix of WHATever and whatEVER attitude with us into our spiritual marriage with Jesus Christ. To some things that He asks, we say, "WhatEVER the Lord asks, I will do." But on other things we think, "WHATever. If I don't do what He asks, it's no big deal. After all He is a forgiving God."

Now here's the bad news/good news reality. Bad news: EVERY act of disobedience to Jesus is spiritual adultery. Good news: Jesus doesn't divorce us for these acts of adulterous disobedience. In fact Peter reminds us of God's infinite patience: "The Lord is not slow in keeping his promise [i.e, God is not in a hurry to execute judgment on the wicked], as some understand slowness. Instead he is patient with you, not wanting anyone to perish, but everyone to come to repentance." 2 Peter 3:9

Really?

Think about it. Doesn't any sin, no matter how insignificant we consider it be, require Jesus' death on the cross to forgive? That sounds pretty significant to me! Too often we place sins on a naughty chart. Little sins are those like lying, gossiping, or lustful looks. Big sins include adultery, murder and felony theft.

The Whatever Factor

Jesus doesn't have such a chart categorizing little and big sins, although in the Old Testament we do find varying forms of punishment that Israelite leaders were instructed to inflict. Paul wrote, "The wages of sin is death." Romans 6:23. Any sin is worthy unto death either for us or Jesus. If we are unrepentant, then the wages of our sin is our eternal death. If repentant, then Jesus' death redeems us from our death penalty and gives us eternal life with Him.

Our discussion would be irrelevant if Paul had written, "The wages of big sins is death, but the little ones are no big deal." Now, some sins might be more egregious to God (like pride: Psalm 10:4, or harming a child: Matthew 18:6), but the death penalty is the same. God doesn't have a "venial" versus "mortal" category for sins—as do Catholics.[20]

As a reference point, what was the "great" sin of Adam and Eve? Adultery? Murder? Felony theft? No. It was simply disobedience: "Don't eat of that tree." The penalty for their "little" disobedience was eternal death against which Jesus promised a Deliverer. The apostle Paul reminds us that "as by [the disobedience of] one man sin entered into the world, and death by sin." Romans 5:12

Satan's temptation to Adam and Eve was: "This is not a big whatEVER mortal sin but just a little venial WHATever one. After all, God is merciful AND even He makes unreasonable demands at times, go ahead and eat. No big deal."

But that seemingly simple act of disobedience has resulted in millenniums of misery, not to forget the death of Jesus.

I once had a girl in my church youth group with the gift of leadership. Other kids just naturally wanted to follow her lead. I wanted to develop her in to an effective spiritual leader.

---

[20] In Roman Catholic theology a mortal, serious, or grave sin is the knowing and willful violation of God's law in a serious matter, for example, idolatry, adultery, murder, slander. Venial sins are are said to be slight sins which do not break our friendship with God, although they injure it.

Problem was, she had a WHATever attitude toward sleeping around with guys.

"But don't you realize this breaks the heart of God and can have eternal consequences?" I pleaded.

She responded with a shrug and tilt of her head: "Oh, it's no big deal. All I have to do is ask God for forgiveness and then everything will be okay."

If that girl chooses to maintain that WHATever attitude toward this sin (and most likely toward other sins in her life), I can't quite picture God welcoming her into heaven with, "My dear child, I know you don't have much interest in pleasing Me nor in having a loving relationship with Me, but since you in all sincerity accepted Me as your Lord and Savior at a youth rally on the evening of July 22, 1973, then heaven is yours. I just hope that your WHATever attitude will someday change for the better. Until that happens we will have to quarantine you to that dark area of heaven where there is weeping and gnashing of teeth. (We'll discuss this "dark area of heaven" in the next chapter.) Saints who, because of their faithfulness on earth, were rewarded by being given seats of judgment will be in charge of your neighborhood. As they see your attitude improve then we'll integrate you into the brighter more joyful neighborhoods of heaven."

I HOPE that last paragraph rubbed you wrong. Aren't you thinking: "There's got to be a better picture of heaven and what is necessary to live there eternally."

Be certain, there is.

There Is No WHATever Sin

There is no such thing as an insignificant WHATever sin. Any sin is spiritual adultery, with the potential of killing our marriage relationship with God.

No, I don't believe God divorces us the moment we disobey. But our disobedient attitude is like a spiritual cancer that can, if not arrested and reversed by the transforming power of God's Spirit, grow and destroy our commitment to Jesus, resulting in our eternal destruction.

Decades ago I heard of an old Indian metaphor that helped me understand the long-term danger of having a WHATever response to God's convictions. Here it is: Your conscience is like a triangle in your fleshy soul. At first the three points are well defined and sharp. Every time you sin that triangle turns in your soul and those sharp edges "prick" you. That's why you feel very uncomfortable with your initial decisions to disregard God's promptings.

But every time you violate your conscience, the triangle turns and turns. Over time, if we continue to violate our conscience, those edges wear down until they are almost smooth and hardly bothersome. That triangle has become like a smooth, turning wheel, but it gradually becomes unnoticeable.

Mark 3:9 warns us to avoid sinning against the Holy Spirit. Christians call that the unpardonable sin. What sin could possibly be worse than David committing adultery with Bathsheba and then instructing his military general to put Bathsheba's husband on the front line of an attack to be murdered on the battle lines? What is worse than Peter denying His Lord three times at the very moment when Christ most needed his support? What could be so bad that Jesus' prayer on the cross, "Father forgive them for they don't know what they are doing", could not cover it?

I don't think any sin is unpardonable. Rather, the unpardonable sin is the sin for which we feel no need to seek pardon. We may have felt the Spirit's conviction or guilt for a while, but after continually turning a deaf ear to the Spirit we lose the ability to feel guilt. In fact, many come to a point where they actually believe that their sin is no longer sin. The apostle Paul describes such in Romans 1, rearranged for brevity:

> Although they know God's righteous decree
> that those who do such things deserve death,

they did not think it worthwhile to retain the knowledge of God, so God gave them over to a depraved mind, so that they do what ought not to be done. They have become filled with every kind of wickedness, evil, greed and depravity. They are full of envy, murder, strife, deceit and malice. They are gossips, slanderers, God-haters, insolent, arrogant and boastful; they invent ways of doing evil; they disobey their parents; they have no understanding, no fidelity, no love, no mercy. They not only continue to do these very things but also approve of those who practice them.

It's as if these folks' practice of sinning has so deadened their consciences they come to believe that what they are doing is acceptable. That is a good definition of the unpardonable sin. Sadly, it's becoming increasingly descriptive of our culture.

God Is a Lover, Not a Bookkeeper

In the 1980s, while pastoring in the beautiful Shenandoah Valley in Virginia, I invited a woman to give a seminar at our church. I had never heard her but others strongly recommended her, so I extended the invitation. (It was a learning moment for me: Never invite a guest speaker/teacher without firsthand knowledge of their theology.)

In the midst of her second presentation, I got the distinct impression that she believed that one could not be saved unless every known sin had been confessed. I publicly challenged her and discovered that my impression was correct.

So I asked: "Let's say Joe is generally a loving, growing Christian but far from perfect. He loves Jesus and loves seeing the positive transformation in his personality that the Spirit is accomplishing. But one evening he gets into a big angry shouting match with his wife. He says some things that are leftovers from his brash, cursing, angry past.

"He storms out the door, throws himself into his car, and slams the door. He starts the engine, revs it up and then lays a strip of rubber on the concrete as he blasts down his long driveway. He hardly slows as he swerves onto the county road. There's a screech of tires as the oncoming dump truck driver makes a futile attempt to avoid Joe, but there's no way. The dump truck slams into Joe's car, crushing him into a mangled mass of metal. Joe is instantly killed.

"Now, ma'am, would you say that since Joe had no time to confess his sins of anger and cursing that he is a lost man?"

Her answer: "Yes, Joe would be lost because there would be unconfessed and unforgiven sins on his heavenly record. But what I think a loving God would do is give Joe a split second of consciousness just before he died where he could offer a quick prayer of confession."

"Well, ma'am," I responded, "evidently I serve a different God than you, because my God is not a punitive bookkeeper. He's a lover. Like a loving marital spouse, which I am privileged to have on earth, God is my spiritual spouse and doesn't stop loving me, nor does He lock the doors to His heavenly home just because I had a momentary relapse into sin. Most marriages, where there has been a growing pattern of love and care, don't rise or fall upon one unpleasant disagreement.

"The same is true of God," I continued. "I believe God's love and grace is broad and wise enough to look upon the whole tenure of my life, rather than a specific good deed or bad. Sure there will be ups and downs; times and seasons of life when I feel close to God and other times when I am pretty aloof or even angry with Him. But He knows my heart. He knows my inner longings. Like Jesus said to the woman caught in adultery, 'I do not condemn you. Now go and live a new, improved life.'"

Bottom line: God is not like Santa Claus, checking His list and checking it twice to see if you've been naughty or nice—before offering you His gift of heaven. He is your spiritual loving spouse. He WANTS to find ways to get you to heaven, rather than digging up excuses to keep you out.

However, Jesus does not reward you with heaven *because* you did enough good deeds nor because you had a moment of conversion. He invites you to heaven because He knows your gratitude for His crucifixion gift and sees your willingness to have the Holy Spirit transform your heart and soul to reflect more of His character which results in your growing desire for His fellowship.

Thus, the invitation to heaven is logical. An unwarranted awesome gift of love, but nevertheless logical. People who love each other should live together. People who don't love each other should not be forced to live together.

I expect a loving God to say, "I'm so grateful that you have not only accepted my love gift of Calvary's forgiveness but your love for Me is growing. You are allowing me to transform your whole character. Your joy in being in fellowship with Me is growing AND (Have you ever thought about this?) I'm finding more joy in fellowship with you. We're becoming kindred spirits. Thus, I would like to invite you to heaven where our love relationship can grow forever without the impediments of sin, pain and death."[21]

Thus the eternal question is not:

"Have you uttered the proper conversion formula?" nor

"Have you confessed every sin?" nor

"Have you done enough good deeds to be worthy of heaven?" nor

"Have you become perfect, with no trace of any sin in your life?"

---

[21] As I noted in Chapter 3, God will not take anyone to heaven who doesn't want to go. Meaning? He won't take anyone who isn't finding a growing joy in knowing, loving and pleasing God in this life because it shows that they won't enjoy fellowship with Him forever. Why should He force someone to live with Him forever who doesn't enjoy His fellowship?

No!

The only relevant questions will be:

"Are you developing a whatEVER attitude toward Me?"

"Is your love for me growing?"

"Are you finding your greatest joy in loving, serving and pleasing me?"

And God's attitude toward our imperfection is best stated by David: "My sacrifice, O God, is a broken spirit; a broken and contrite heart you, God, *will not despise.*" Psalm 51:17

A broken and contrite heart is a whatEVER heart, changing one from in the inside out into a true child of God. However, Charles Stanley suggests that there will be a dark neighborhood in heaven for any Christian whose spirit is far from contrite and broken.

Really? Yes. Read on.

Imagination Station #6

God does have a sense of humor.
Have you ever read the first chapter of Ezekiel? Try it.
I think God may have given Ezekiel a glimpse of heaven AS IT REALLY IS. Not in earth-like images as shown to John the Revelator: a walled city, streets, a temple and thrones.
Rather, Ezekiel got a glimpse of something from heaven, which he tries to describe in earthly terms. But the best he can do is say, "Well, it's LIKE that... but it's really not."
Go ahead, read Ezekiel's first chapter and prepare to smile.
Count how many times he says something looked "like" or "as if" or "as though." I found fourteen of these words/phrases in my Living Bible. Obviously, he's trying to describe something for which he has no meaningful counterpart on earth. (Maybe that's why UFO enthusiasts—myself not included—think he saw an Unidentified Flying Object!)
This does help us understand why in the Bible God describes heaven as something we would desire on earth, only much MUCH better than mere relief, security, and honor. "Do you desire these things now? In heaven you'll receive these a hundred times over."
But in Ezekiel's vision God challenges us to imagine that heaven is light years beyond what we see, hear, and experience on earth.

Section III:
Heavenly Rewards

Chapter 7:

The Dark Side of Heaven

A "dark side" to heaven? According to Dr. Charles Stanley: "To be in the 'outer darkness' is to be in the kingdom of God but outside the circle of men and women whose faithfulness on this earth earned them a special rank or position of authority." *Eternal Security*, pg. 126.

We'll begin this section on heavenly rewards in the darkness and then move into the light. That might seem unusual, so stay with me.

I have never thought of heaven as having a bright, happy section *and* a dark, suffering section... until I read Charles Stanley's idea that one could make it to heaven but end up in the "outer darkness" neighborhood where there is weeping and gnashing of teeth. It got me to wondering: Could the reverse also be to true in Stanley's perception of hell. Could there be a "temperate neighborhood" in hell where life is really quite bearable?[22]

---

[22] I add this sentence merely for comparative logical thinking. However, I believe the Bible offers a concept of hell fire that differs from that held by the majority of Christians.

This light and dark, happy and sad concept of heaven is the result of the Evangelical's attempt to make sense of heavenly "rewards" which teaches that the holier your life, the greater your reward in heaven. This is inevitably what happens when an erroneous primary doctrine like security-of-salvation is embraced. On the surface, some texts "seem" to support it—plus, it feels good. But every primary doctrine has related secondary doctrines that must be harmonized with one's primary doctrine. When attempting to harmonize those secondary doctrines with an erroneous primary doctrine, strange and weird explanations are often championed.

The security-of-salvation concept is one of the Evangelical's banner doctrines of God's grace. However, when one tries to harmonize it with the secondary doctrine of heavenly rewards, then things don't feel so good. The idea of a dark side of heaven is such a "don't-feel-so-good" AND "doesn't-make-much-sense" doctrine. So let's look at the texts.

Earning Heavenly Rewards

Jesus' parable of the servants utilizing the talents their master loaned them is one textual basis for the rewards concept.[23] The more faithful and creative their use of their master's talents, the greater was their reward upon his return. But the lack of courage of the third servant to invest and increase his master's talents brought rebuke:

> Then he who had received the one talent came and said, "Lord, I knew you to be a hard man, reaping where you have not sown, and gathering where you have not scattered seed. And I was afraid, and went and hid your talent in the ground. Look, there you have what is yours."

---

[23] Matthew 25:15-30 (NKJV) – Parable of the Three Servants

> But his lord answered and said to him, "You wicked and lazy servant, you knew that I reap where I have not sown, and gather where I have not scattered seed. So you ought to have deposited my money with the bankers, and at my coming I would have received back my own with interest. Therefore take the talent from him, and give it to him who has ten talents. For to everyone who has, more will be given, and he will have abundance; but from him who does not have, even what he has will be taken away." And cast the unprofitable servant into the outer darkness. There will be weeping and gnashing of teeth. Matthew 25:24-30 (NKJV)

Evangelicals would say that the faithful use of one's talents (holy living) does not determine your salvation, but must determine something. Stanley suggests that it determines which heavenly neighborhood you'll inherit: dark or bright and your status in each of these. And how could Stanley come up with the dreadful idea of there being a dark, sad neighborhood in heaven? Think about it.

If Stanley is allowing people into heaven who accepted Christ yet later become not only unbelievers but, as Jesus said, "wicked" then they CANNOT be allowed into the same heavenly neighborhood as the faithful believers. They will need a holding place where they can be rehabilitated into kingdom people. The Catholics used to call that place "Purgatory," but Stanley calls it the "outer darkness" neighborhood.

Evidently Stanley believes that people who choose not to live a life of faith after conversion and not to be spiritually mature will end up in that dark area of heaven called "outer darkness where there will be weeping and gnashing of teeth." In fact, it seems that the only difference between these "outer darkness" saints and some folks in hell is that even though their

The Whatever Factor

characters and behavior are similar, the "outer darkness" saints fortunately had a sincere "I accept Jesus as my Lord and Savior" moment which guaranteed their ticket to heaven.

This dark portion of heaven evidently would also be the dwelling place for the believing Christians who had a WHATever attitude toward becoming a disciple of Jesus in both character and behavior. Evidently the purpose of this "outer darkness" neighborhood is for their rehabilitation of faith and to develop a character that would be compatible and safe for the other saints. It is assumed that at the appropriate stage of their rehabilitation they will be introduced to the holy saints in the bright, happy portion of heaven. If they pass the test, then the heavenly moving van will pull up to their dark door and transport them to the bright side of heaven where there is no night.

Remember Charles Stanley's proclamation: "Discipleship has nothing to do with whether you will go to heaven or not.... It is possible to be a child of God and never a disciple of Christ. We can live the Christian life with the assurance of heaven as our ultimate destiny but miss the process of maturing as a disciple." *Handbook for Christian Living*, p. 505.

Follow carefully as I connect the Evangelical dots.

First dot: If one believes that salvation is secure and irrevocable at the moment of sincere conversion, then...

Second dot: A person will be saved even if they in later life revoke their belief in God, thus...

Third dot: This "fallen away" Christian would be taken to heaven even though they have no faith relationship with Jesus Christ, so...

Fourth dot: It makes sense that Stanley is obliged to create an "outer darkness" neighborhood in heaven for these "wicked" yet saved unbelievers.

Although I recognize Stanley's theological consistency, the articulation of such makes me cringe. As such, I will let him explain it. In regards to the "wicked and lazy servant" who was cast into "outer darkness" he writes:

The final verse of this parable is so severe that many commentators assume it is a description of hell. It is not. . . Where is this place represented by the "outer darkness" in Jesus' parable? To be in the "outer darkness" is to be in the kingdom of God but outside the circle of men and women whose faithfulness on this earth earned them a special rank or position of authority. *Eternal Security,* pp. 124-126.

My difficulty with Stanley's explanation is threefold: (1) This was a "wicked" servant, so how can Stanley say he will be in heaven? (2) The servant was cast out from the presence of the Master (symbolically away from the presence of God), into outer darkness, the biblical description of being lost. (3) It is revealing how Evangelical preachers proclaim the believer's salvation as "pure grace" (free irrevocable gift), but their heavenly rewards as being earned (works based religion). Like Stanley says, rewards are dispensed by God because their "faithfulness on this earth **earned** them a special rank or position of authority."

What *Are* Heavenly Rewards?

And what is the result of maturing as a disciple according to Stanley? Evidently, in addition to living on the bright side of heaven, it is rewards of rulership and other goodies.

This concept of heavenly rewards has always puzzled me. What could these rewards be? Surely it is more than moving from the "outer darkness" section into the more upscale happy neighborhood of heaven. Will I be a ruler over hundreds of people—or three? Will I live in the upper class section of the Holy City—or in the country with the farmers? Will I live on the streets of gold—or on the lanes of dust and mud? Will my "mansion" be large—or a studio apartment? Will I wear heavenly jewels on my crown—or just a crown of leaves?

Without wishing to sound sacrilegious, I find myself thinking: *Who really cares! I imagine ALL of heaven as paradise, so just getting in the gate is reward enough for me.* I assume we will all walk on the streets of gold, all sing with the angel choir, all have beautiful homes, all have personal time with the Almighty, and all enjoy being hugged by Jesus. So why do I need other incentives? And if there are "classes" of saints in heaven, might that create jealousy?

AND—truth be told—after pastoring for over forty years, I really have no driving desire to be a ruler or administrator over a crowd of people forever.

"So, don't you believe there is ANY distinction of rewards for the saints?" you may ask. The only reward I can understand is one that comes by "common experience." Meaning what? Let me explain in Chapter Nine.

First, however, in the next chapter let's look at the biblical evolution of the heavenly rewards concept.

Imagination Station #7

So heaven is a special place of **relief, security,** and **togetherness** with Jesus. But as a persistent child might ask, "Yes, I'm really excited about seeing grandma and grandpa, but what are we going to DO there?"

In Corinthians, Paul writes: "Eye hath not seen, nor ear heard, neither have entered into the heart of man, the things which God hath prepared for them that love him." 1 Corinthians 2:9 (KJV)

Paul was describing the power of God's spirit transforming us beyond anything ever known. But I doubt he would be upset if we also applied that same concept to heaven: "You have never seen anything, nor heard anything, nor even imagined anything close to what God has in store for you in heaven."

Heaven will engage sensory capabilities for which we have no comparison: sounds and harmonies never before heard, physical and mental abilities never experienced except in the minutest manner. Even today's neurologists tell us that we use only about 10% of our brain (some folks a lot less than that!) and this the degenerate brain of humans after thousands of years of sin. Imagine utilizing all of one's brain and senses and then having God recreate our brains to their expanded capacity of His original creation!

The best way to illustrate our sensory limitations is limited examples. For example, how would you explain the beauty, the subtle colors and delicate texturing of a rose to a person who was born blind? One who has never seen colors, shades or shadows... no person, place, or thing. Or how would you explain to a deaf person the beauty of music, of many voices praising God, the melody of the keyboard, the suave sound of a mellow trumpet, or the delicate sound of the harp?

If we have nothing on earth to which we can compare heaven, how can we imagine what it will be like? We can do what God did for the biblical peoples, i.e., imagine the best thing on earth and then grasp that heaven will be a bazillion times better. The best for many in Jesus' day were homes, vineyards, no pain, no death and being respected/honored. So God portrayed heaven in these terms.

*Now stretch your imagination. Embrace **new** possibilities.*

Chapter 8:

Living Under an Old or New Testament Concept of Heavenly Rewards

✟

"If anyone desires to be first, he shall be last of all and servant of all." Jesus

Good parents understand how child training goes through different phases.

You do things differently when they grow from childhood into maturity. When but a child of three years, little Johnny is punished for lying to his mother. Whatever the form of punishment, it is intended to teach Johnny that lying is unacceptable behavior in that family. Mother may try to explain some of the reasons why lying is unacceptable, understanding that, at his age, Johnny is unable to fully comprehend the deeper reasons. He does understand cause and effect: thus lying is rewarded with punishment.

However, mother hopes that Johnny will mature to eventually internalize good moral principles. She hopes he will eventually choose not to lie, not because it might bring punishment but, because lying destroys trust which is essential for building loving relationships with family, friends, and with Johnny's future spouse.

There is an imperfect but similar comparison between how people responded to God in the Old Testament versus the New. In the Old Testament God's people were referred to and treated like "children." After four hundred years and multiple generations of living under the heavy hand of Egyptian slavery, the children of Israel were often incapable of understanding the deeper reasons for God's commands.

So, on Mt. Sinai God gave them the Ten Commandments and a host of other do's and don'ts. He said that, if they disobeyed, they would be rewarded with punishment. If they obeyed, they would be rewarded with honor, power, and goodies. Specifically, they would be rewarded with a "Promised Land flowing with milk and honey." They also would be rewarded with a national position of honor and rule over all nations of the earth. All nations would come to Israel seeking to understand and benefit from their wisdom, wealth and power. In return, the Israelites would tell them that these blessings came as a reward for obeying the great "I Am. The God of Abraham, Isaac and Jacob" and would encourage all nations to follow suit.

However, in the teachings of Jesus and the writings of Paul, Peter, and John, we begin to see a shift, not only in one's reason for obeying God but also in the concept of heavenly rewards. New followers of Christ, who previously had been taught the do's and don'ts of Yahweh as though they were children with rewards of "a land flowing with milk and honey" plus the prospect of being powerful world leaders, are now challenged to "grow up" and become mature in their spiritual understanding and motivations.

They are now being charged—not with do's and don'ts—but with character transformation, to have the mind of Christ. The result? Well, on earth their rewards would often be that of suffering and hardship, but in heaven an eternal fellowship with Jesus.

Here are some examples:

1. Jesus speaking to his disciples:

> I still have many things to say to you, but you cannot bear them now. However, when He, the Spirit of truth, has come, He will guide you into all truth. John 16:12-13 (NKJV)

The disciples still had an immature mistaken Old Testament view of the kingdom wherein Jesus would overthrow the Romans and reestablish Israel as the ruling nation of the world AND the disciples would be rewarded by being appointed rulers in this new kingdom. They were not yet ready to receive the New Testament reality that Jesus' kingdom was not of this world, and that they must first suffer many things.

2. Earthly rewards of hardship:

> Dear friends, do not be surprised at the fiery ordeal that has come on you to test you, as though something strange were happening to you. But rejoice inasmuch as you participate in the sufferings of Christ, so that you may be overjoyed when his glory is revealed. 1 Peter 4:12,13

> Then the mother of Zebedee's sons came to Him with her sons, kneeling down and asking something from Him. And He said to her, "What do you wish?" She said to Him, "Grant that these two sons of mine may sit, one on Your right hand and the other on the left, in Your kingdom.

> But Jesus answered and said, "You do not know what you ask. Are you able to drink the cup that I am about to drink, and be baptized with the baptism that I am baptized with? Matthew 20: 20-22 (NKJV)

The mother of James and John was the career promotional agent for her sons. She was the first to ask what all the disciples thought and wished, that her sons might sit in the positions of honor and power on each side of Jesus. This is very similar to Christians believing that their faithful obedience will be rewarded by their being placed on heavenly thrones to rule.

3. But it's time to grow up:

> And I, brethren, could not speak to you as to spiritual people but as to carnal, as to babes in Christ. I fed you with milk and not with solid food; for until now you were not able to receive it, and even now you are still not able; for you are still carnal. For where there are envy, strife, and divisions among you, are you not carnal and behaving like mere men? 1 Corinthians 3:1-3 (NKJV)

Paul, wishing to speak to the Corinthians as men of maturity, finds that they still are spiritual children:

> Now these are the gifts Christ gave to the church: the apostles, the prophets, the evangelists, and the pastors and teachers. Their responsibility is to equip God's people to do his work and build up the church, the body of Christ. This will continue until we all come to such unity in our faith and knowledge of God's Son that we will be

mature in the Lord, measuring up to the full and complete standard of Christ. Then we will no longer be immature like children. We won't be tossed and blown about by every wind of new teaching. We will not be influenced when people try to trick us with lies so clever they sound like the truth. Instead, we will speak the truth in love, growing in every way more and more like Christ, who is the head of his body, the church. Ephesians 4:11-15 (NLT)

4. In this maturation process, rewards that His followers once expected (e.g. honor, power and goodies), are being redefined by Jesus as a life of service:

And when He was in the house He asked them [disciples], 'What was it you disputed among yourselves on the road?' But they kept silent, for on the road they had disputed among themselves who would be the greatest. And He sat down, called the twelve, and said to them, 'If anyone desires to be first, he shall be last of all and servant of all.' Then He took a little child and set him in the midst of them. And when He had taken him in His arms, He said to them, 'Whoever receives one of these little children in My name receives Me; and whoever receives Me, receives not Me but Him who sent Me.' Mark 9:33-37 (NKJV)

5. In the New Testament the heavenly reward of fellowship with Jesus is lifted up:

> Do not let your hearts be troubled. You believe in God; believe also in me. My Father's house has many rooms; if that were not so, would I have told you that I am going there to prepare a place for you? And if I go and prepare a place for you, I will come back and take you to be with me that you also may be where I am. John 14:1-3

> I saw the Holy City, the new Jerusalem, coming down out of heaven from God, prepared as a bride beautifully dressed for her husband. And I heard a loud voice from the throne saying, 'Look! God's dwelling place is now among the people, and he will dwell with them. They will be his people, and God himself will be with them and be their God. He will wipe every tear from their eyes. There will be no more death nor mourning or crying or pain, for the old order of things has passed away.' Revelation 21:1-4

What is Jesus saying will be your reward for obedience? Not so much the glory of sitting on a throne and having servants tend to your every whim, but rather the opportunity to serve and suffer for Him on earth and then to enjoy fellowship face-to-face with Him and serve in heaven. Wow! That is a major reward paradigm shift. This doesn't mean that we won't be given leadership responsibility in heaven, but it completely changes the picture of what that role might entail.

6. But didn't Jesus promise hundredfold rewards to Peter:

> Then answered Peter and said unto him, "Behold, we have forsaken all, and followed thee; what shall we have therefore?" And Jesus said unto them, "Verily I say unto you, that ye which have followed me, in the regeneration when the Son of man shall sit in the throne of his glory, ye also shall sit upon twelve thrones, judging the twelve tribes of Israel. And every one that hath forsaken houses, or brethren, or sisters, or father, or mother, or wife, or children, or lands, for my name's sake, shall receive an hundredfold, and shall inherit everlasting life." Matthew 19:27-29 (KJV)

Well, that sounds pretty straightforward, you may think. Their rewards were to sit on thrones and judge the nations, right?

The Old Testament idea of sitting on a throne meant that you had many servants who would bow and serve you in every manner. Is that similar to what you believe, that your reward will be a throne upon which you can sit and rule? Do you envision other saints bowing and serving your every need?

Forgive my satire but who are these "lowly" saints serving you? Might they be those who are given green card work visas from the zone of "outer darkness" in order to serve the more righteous? Could their servitude be part of their rehabilitation into becoming fully qualified disciples who someday will graduate from the "outer darkness" region into the constant daylight atmosphere of that part of heaven in which you live? But what will happen when all of the "outer darkness" residents finally graduate in the kingdom of light. Who, then, will do the servant work for all who are ruling from thrones?

Do you want to be rewarded in heaven with a throne and leadership responsibility? If that is one of the rewards in heaven, then drop any earthly notion that it entails honor, glory and being served. Instead, switch the picture to Jesus' example of what a leader does, i.e. kneeling, serving, sacrificing for others, and putting others first in everything.

Are you still interested? If so, understand that your servant training program is the here and now by kneeling and serving like Jesus.

The New Testament Roll of a Ruler

The Old Testament contrasted the rolls and privileges of a ruler versus a servant. However, in the New Testament Jesus introduces the concept of rewards whereby to rule is to function as a servant.

As Bill Hybels writes in his book Descending into Greatness (1994), the New Testament formula for becoming great is to step down, down, down from thinking highly of ourselves, deserving of honor and praise from others, to bowing to our knees and serving the lowliest of humankind. Jesus illustrated this "descending into greatness" by his own example of leaving His heavenly throne and taking on the form of a human shuffling along the dusty pathways of a sinful world. He exhibited this servanthood by kneeling to wash His disciples' feet. He taught it when he said:"If anyone desires to be first, he shall be last of all and servant of all." Mark 9:35 (NKJV)

Evidently the New Testament concept of sitting on thrones is redefined as that of a humble servant. Maybe it means spending most of one's time off the throne, stepping down and doing the dirty work of a servant for the people one leads. Jesus did that. He showed us that ruling in the kingdom sense is taking on the attitude of a servant, bowing on our hands and knees, and doing the work of a servant.

Maybe it's similar to the reverse pyramid job work ethic. Those who are at the top of the pyramid should not think about how they deserve more pay, perks, and people waiting on them hand and foot. Rather, when the pyramid is turned upside down, these "rulers, leaders, managers" are now on the bottom which means that their leadership takes the form of a servant. They are now responsible for serving and enhancing the lives of all of the people whom they supervise. Their job is to make each employee on his/her team feel like the most valuable person.

With this New Testament concept of being rewarded with leadership as being synonymous with getting on our knees and serving, then are you still interested? Are you first in line jumping up and down, calling out, "Pick me! Pick me!"?

Let's do a heart check. The Bible describes most of those whom God chose to lead as people who were not waving their arms with "Pick me!" Instead, their common response was, "Why have you chosen me for I am SO undeserving and unqualified?" Some examples:

> Moses: "And Moses said unto the Lord, 'O my Lord, I am not eloquent, neither heretofore, nor since thou hast spoken unto thy servant: but I am slow of speech, and of a slow tongue.'" Exodus 4:10 (KJV)

> Isaiah: "Then said I, 'Woe is me! for I am undone; because I am a man of unclean lips, and I dwell in the midst of a people of unclean lips.'" Isaiah 6:5 (NKJV)

> Saul: "And Saul answered and said, 'Am not I a Benjamite, of the smallest of the tribes of Israel? And my family the least of all the families of the tribe of Benjamin? Wherefore then speakest thou so to me?'" 1 Samuel 9:21 (KJV)

In contrast, Jesus warned that at the judgment many who present their righteous deeds credentials with the expectation of significant heavenly rewards will be gravely disappointed.

> Jesus' response was sobering: "Many will say to me in that day, 'Lord, Lord, have we not prophesied in thy name? and in thy name have cast out devils? and in thy name done many wonderful works?' And then will I profess unto them, 'I never knew you: depart from me, ye that work iniquity.'" Matthew 7:22-23 (KJV)

As one follows the trajectory of Scripture, it becomes increasingly obvious that heavenly rewards look less and less like the Old Testament childish concept of "getting honor and goodies" and more and more like the servant life of Jesus.

The Apostle Paul displays more than any other biblical writer what it means to be called by God to be a leader. Paul gave up EVERYTHING for the honor of serving and suffering for Christ. "I count all things but loss for the excellency of the knowledge of Christ Jesus my Lord: for whom I have suffered the loss of all things, and do count them but dung, that I may win Christ." Philippians 3:8 (KJV)

Paul became all things to all people in order to win some: "Though I am free and belong to no one, I have made myself a slave to everyone, to win as many as possible." 1 Corinthians 9:19

Is there any other way of understanding the biblical promise of heavenly rewards than simply "thrones and goodies"? Yes, I believe there is a sensible and beautiful concept which I'll discuss in the next chapter. But, first, let me explain that phrase I just used: the trajectory of Scripture.

Defining the "Trajectory" of Scripture

Ever hear the phrase, "Well, we've come full circle"? Scripture does that also. I call it the "trajectory of Scripture."

Merriam-Webster Dictionary: tra·jec·to·ry: "The curved path along which something (such as an artillery shell) moves through the air or through space."

Today's modern artillery crews now can fire several rounds within a minute, then tuck their cannon back into its mount and scoot to another location. Why? Because opposing artillery crews can track by computer the incoming shells AND from what location they were fired. All this before the incoming shells make impact.

The opposing crew can then fire their cannon on a reverse track back to the first artillery emplacement within seconds. That's why it's so critical for today's artillery crews to "shoot and scoot" if they hope to survive.

The ability of the computer to project not only where a round will land but also track its trajectory back to the source is similar to what we see in Scripture. Some biblical practices and teachings have lofty origins in the book of Genesis, then deviate through the centuries from God's ideal as recorded in the Old Testament, then come back in line with God's plan through the teachings of Jesus and other New Testament writers. I believe the concept of heavenly rewards follows such a trajectory. Let me illustrate with four examples: slavery, women, divorce, and polygamy.

Trajectory #1: Slavery

It is obvious in the first chapters of Genesis that God created man and woman as equals, although each would serve different roles. The concept of slavery was irrelevant because there was no sin, no desire for one person to control or own another. And no hint that one should rule over the other.

Then we launch into the fall. Cain kills Abel and in a few chapters we have war. Among other painful results, conquered peoples are forced into slavery by their captors. By the Book of Exodus we find the Israelites have suffered as slaves for several hundred years. By then it was a common practice among all nations to bring captives home to serve as slaves. The conditions under which a slave lived generally were very cruel and demeaning. Thus, in a few biblical pages, the trajectory of slavery has gone from all people being created equal to cruel masters driving slaves under the whip till they die.

But, after the Israelites were delivered from their Egyptian slavery and began their march toward their Promised Land, God gave them new guidelines for a more honorable treatment of slaves. It was assumed that, after conquering the peoples of Canaan and possessing the land, the Israelites would need to know how to humanely treat their new Canaanite slaves. So, along with the Ten Commandments, God (from Mt. Sinai) gave to Israel new slavery guidelines which can be found in the books of Exodus and Leviticus. Here's an example: "An owner who knocks out the tooth of a male or female slave must let the slave go free to compensate for the tooth." Exodus 21:27

Although the slave is still referred to as "property," this new guideline is a major step in the trajectory back toward treating a slave as a human being rather than merely a possession. Can you imagine such a law back in Pharaoh's Egypt—letting an Israelite slave go free if his Egyptian master knocked his tooth out?

You might ask, "Why didn't God immediately correct the slavery problem by issuing laws forbidding the Israelites to even own slaves?" I'll leave that answer to those who wish to debate the pros and cons of making immediate sweeping societal changes versus making those changes in a graduated manner over time. What we do see here is God charging His people to lead the way in improving human rights. God begins to nudge the trajectory of slavery back toward the concept of dignity, equality, and freedom.

Then, leap forward to the New Testament book of Philemon 1:8-19. Notice in the following narrative that Paul is encouraging Philemon to treat his slave, Onesimus, as a brother in Christ. In fact, Paul says "treat him in the same manner as you would treat me."

> Therefore, although in Christ I could be bold and order you to do what you ought to do, yet I prefer to appeal to you on the basis of love. It is as none other than Paul—an old man and now also a prisoner of Christ Jesus—that I appeal to you for my son Onesimus, who became my son while I was in chains. Formerly he was useless to you, but now he has become useful both to you and to me.
>
> I am sending him—who is my very heart—back to you. I would have liked to keep him with me so that he could take your place in helping me while I am in chains for the gospel. But I did not want to do anything without your consent, so that any favor you do would not seem forced but would be voluntary. Perhaps the reason he was separated from you for a little while was that you might have him back forever— no longer as a slave, but better than a slave, as a dear brother. He is very dear to me but even dearer to you, both as a fellow man and as a brother in the Lord.

The Whatever Factor

> So if you consider me a partner, welcome him as you would welcome me. If he has done you any wrong or owes you anything, charge it to me. I, Paul, am writing this with my own hand. I will pay it back—not to mention that you owe me your very self.

No, Paul hasn't gone so far as to tell Philemon not to own a slave, but it is strongly implied as Paul gives to Philemon the same lesson he gave to the Galatians: "There is neither Jew nor Gentile, neither slave nor free, nor is there male and female, for you are all one in Christ Jesus." Galatians 3:28

Paul has articulated the equality of each human as God instituted in Genesis. Over biblical time God has nudged the trajectory of slavery back to His creation ideal: all of His children are created "free" and equal.

Trajectory #2: Women

God created Adam and Eve free and equal, as symbolized within the creation story. God took a rib from Adam and built around it a new and different being. He didn't take a bone from Adam's head, because she was not to rule over him. Nor did He take a bone from Adam's foot because she was not to be trampled upon by Adam. Rather, God took a bone from his side... from over his heart... because they were to stand side by side, heart to heart as equals in a loving partnership.

Then the story plunges into the fall of humanity and its accompanying demeaning of women. We find in Old Testament history that women were inhumanely demoted in most societies and wives were considered property.

A father who could not marry his daughter off to a good man (or most any man) was shamed. That unmarried daughter was a constant blemish on her father. A good example of this was when Jacob worked seven years to earn the right to marry

Laban's younger and more attractive daughter, Rachel (Genesis 29). But Laban tricked Jacob on his wedding night and slipped his less attractive and unmarried older daughter Leah into Jacob's tent. Unmarried Leah was an embarrassment to Laban, so by hook or crook he got her married off. Then Jacob had to work seven more years to officially earn Rachel's hand.

Women had few rights. A husband could kick his wife out of his tent simply for "burning his toast" as it were. Where, then, could the wife go? If she went back home to her father she brought great shame upon him. She couldn't remarry because she was still the property of her upset husband. Often rejected women lived together with other women or ended up on the street as prostitutes... merely to survive.

Then we see women's New Testament trajectory back to equality. First, we see Jesus' unusually kind treatment of women as exampled by:

1. The woman caught in adultery whom Jesus shielded from stoning and didn't condemn (John 8).
2. His kind treatment of Mary when she washed His feet with perfume amidst critical stares and comments of other men (Matthew 26).
3. His gracious conversation with the much married and adulterous woman at Jacob's well (John Chapter 4).
4. And His choice of Mary Magdalene, a former prostitute, as the first evangelist of His resurrection:

> Now when Jesus was risen early the first day of the week, he appeared first to Mary Magdalene, out of whom he had cast seven devils. And she went and told them [disciples] that had been with him, as they mourned and wept. And they, when they had heard that he was alive, and had been seen of her, believed not. Mark 16:9-11 (KJV)

And, again, Paul raises the value of women to full recovery in the familiar passage:

> There is neither Jew nor Gentile, neither slave nor free, nor is there male and female, for you are all one in Christ Jesus. If you belong to Christ, then you are Abraham's seed, and heirs according to the promise. Galatians 3:28

Notice here that Paul says women are equal heirs of God's promises. In the very next chapter, Paul goes a step further. In Christ, women are now "sons:"

> But when the fullness of the time was come, God sent forth his Son, made of a woman, made under the law, to redeem them that were under the law, that we might receive the adoption of sons. And because you are sons, God hath sent forth the Spirit of his Son into your hearts, crying, "Abba, Father." Galatians 4:4-6

Who are sons? All whom he just referenced in the third chapter: all Jews, Gentiles, slaves, free, male and female who believe in Christ. Why does Paul say Christian women are "sons"? Because sons were previously the primary inheritor's of property, power, and rights from their father. But now male and female have an equal inheritance. The Genesis equality ideal is being reestablished.

Trajectory #3: Divorce

The pattern for divorce is similar. Every Bible student knows God's original ideal: Adam and Eve. The two shall become one flesh. Then sin, followed by divorce. Men could "put their wife away" for most any reason and we have just noted the dire choices women had for survival.

So what does God do to rebuild the honor and dignity of wives? In Deuteronomy 24 God tells husbands that they must give the rejected wife a "bill of divorcement." Why? Because this was proof that she was no longer "owned" by her husband, but was free to date and remarry. This put an end to the nasty trick of a mean husband kicking out his wife and still claiming ownership of her, thus preventing her from establishing a new home with another man. While God did not immediately condemn divorce, He did take a positive step toward improving the lot of a divorced woman and reinforcing the sanctity of marriage.

Then, again, in the New Testament we find Jesus bringing the trajectory of divorce closer to the Genesis ideal: the two shall become "one flesh"... for life. "I tell you that anyone who divorces his wife, except for sexual immorality, and marries another woman commits adultery." Matthew 19:9

In this one line, Jesus limits the reason for divorce to "sexual immorality," not only further protecting women but also directing our attention back to the Edenic ideal. God wants us to elevate the importance of "becoming one flesh for life."

Trajectory #4: Polygamy

Similar trajectory. God did not create for Adam two or ten wives. Just one. Polygamy or divorce was not intended nor needed. But by Solomon's time even God's chosen leaders had many wives and God did not condemn them. But by the time of Jesus and Paul the trajectory back to one man and one woman is clear.

The Greater Heavenly Reward: Fellowship

I have shared these examples of the trajectory of Scripture to suggest that the idea of heavenly rewards seems to follow a similar pattern. In Eden the greatest reward for Adam and Eve was their fellowship with Jesus as He regularly walked and talked with them in the garden. And their "reward" of rulership was that they had dominion and responsibility in tending the garden and its animals.

In the Old Testament we find God promising to narrow-sighted humans power, goodies, and sitting on thrones as rewards for obedience. Evidently this was the kind of rewards that folks back then could best understand. But in the New Testament we see a growing emphasis of heavenly rewards, not so much as power and goodies but, as the reestablishing and enjoyment of walking and talking with Jesus. Jesus promised: "And if I go and prepare a place for you, I will come again, and receive you unto myself; that where I am, there ye may be also." John 14:3 (KJV)

Yes, He promises to "prepare a place" for us. We think of that as a nice heavenly home. True, but His emphasis is not on the home but on the fellowship: "that where I am there ye may be also.In Eden the fellowship with Jesus was our first parents' greatest reward. And in the last book of the Bible we see Eden restored: "Look! God's dwelling place is now among the people, and he will dwell with them. They will be his people, and God himself will be with them and be their God." Revelation 21:3-4

From Eden to Eden; fellowship to fellowship as the greatest reward.

And the "sitting on thrones" part? Who knows? Maybe that will go back to the Edenic example as well where Adam and Eve were given rulership over God's creation—not over other people. Maybe each of us will be rewarded the privilege and responsibility of a planet or even a whole galaxy to creatively manage, so that its beauty reflects our unique personality and is our way of glorifying God through His creation.

Now, in the next chapter, let me share with you what I believe to be the most beautiful and sensible concept of heavenly rewards: the fellowship gained through common experience.

Imagination Station #8

Some writers claim to have had a dream or vision of heaven. Whether their experiences are genuine and their views of heaven accurate is not important. Bottom line, their descriptions stretch my imagination. One woman writes: "There, when the veil that darkens our vision shall be removed and our eyes shall behold that world of beauty of which we now catch glimpses through the microscope..."

Microscopic vision? In another place she wrote: "I saw a table of pure silver, it was many miles in length, yet our eyes could extent over it." Telescopic vision?

Wow! That is way beyond riding on lions. Imagine that you and your friends are sitting on the grass with Jesus. As He talks about a blade of grass, your microscopic vision has zoomed in like an electron microscope. You can actually see every atom and molecule in movement and transformation. Then He draws your attention to a droplet of water on that blade of grass and asks, "Would you like to go on a journey with me into the universe of the atomic miniature?"

In case you initially hesitate to think about Jesus and you miniaturizing yourselves to travel into a drop of water—kind of like "Honey, I Shrunk the Kids"—this would be no problem for Jesus! Remember He is the omnipresent (everywhere at one time), omnipotent (powerful enough to do anything, including creating and sustaining the cosmos) ruler of all things. Even so, He "miniaturized" Himself to be born in Mary's womb and limited Himself to function as a humble, poor carpenter.

So, whoosh! Miniaturized, you begin your adventure into a drop of water with Jesus as your tour guide. It's SO complex that it may take you hundreds of years. You discover and learn the nature of its electrons and protons and photons and neutrons and pions and muons and kaons and Lambda baryons and neutrinos and charm quarks and bottom quarks and top quarks and tetraquarks and Higgs bosons and weak gauge bosons and gravitons and magnetic monopoles. (And these are only what humans now know about the atom; imagine how much more there must be!) You not only see and learn but actually feel the various energies of each and hear the harmonious music that together they create with their vibrations. Music that sounds like praise to their Creator.

Chapter 9:

The Reward of Common Experience

Would you live a different kind of Christian life if there were no rewards in heaven?

If you believe that your heavenly ticket is secure because you once accepted Jesus but your heavenly rewards must be earned by the measure of your disciplined Christian life would you, then, live a different kind of Christian life if there were **no** rewards in heaven?

Would you live differently if the rewards for everyone are the same and offered as a free gift? If entering the pearly gates, sitting at the feet of Jesus, meeting departed loved ones and living in an eternal atmosphere of love was the ONLY reward? How you answer those questions may be an insight into your motivation.

I was preaching a sermon wherein I challenged the traditional concept of "earned" heavenly rewards of power and goodies. I remember an older couple sitting to my left in the audience slowly shaking their heads in disagreement. Later I approached them in conversation. As we talked he said, "It's just not fair. I believe that when a person has worked hard to live a good life there MUST be rewards for that." Is that also how you feel about rewards?

This concept of heavenly rewards has always puzzled me. Again, let me ask you: If there are heavenly rewards, what might they be? Dr. Stanley says it will be "special rank or position of authority."[24]

> Will you rule over hundreds of people—or three?
>
> Will you dwell in the upper class section of the Holy City—or in the country?
>
> Will you walk on streets of gold—or on the dusty and bumpy road?
>
> Will your "mansion" be large—or a one-room affair?
>
> Will you wear heavenly jewels on your crown—or a wreath of oak leaves?

I sense you're wondering: "So, don't you believe there is ANY distinction of rewards for the saints?" Maybe you conclude that I don't believe in rewards. I do—just not in the traditional sense. So, please, allow your heart to consider how to approach this subject openly and in a search for truth.

Doesn't the Bible promise heavenly rewards? It is true, there are a LOT of texts teaching some form of heavenly rewards. Verses like these (all from the ESV):

---

[24] *Eternal Security*, pg. 126

Matthew 16:27: "For the Son of Man is going to come with his angels in the glory of his Father, and then he will repay each person according to what he has done."

Luke 12:33-34: "Sell your possessions, and give to the needy. Provide yourselves with moneybags that do not grow old, with a treasure in the heavens that does not fail, where no thief approaches and no moth destroys. For where your treasure is, there will your heart be also."

Matthew 25:21: "His master said to him, 'Well done, good and faithful servant. You have been faithful over a little; I will set you over much. Enter into the joy of your master.'"

Revelation 22:12: "Behold, I am coming soon, bringing my recompense with me, to repay everyone for what he has done."

Matthew 6:3-4: "When you give to the needy, do not let your left hand know what your right hand is doing, so that your giving may be in secret. And your Father who sees in secret will reward you."

So the impulsive, traditional conclusion (i.e. "God said it. I believe it. That settles it.") from these texts is this: "If the servant to whom the master gave ten talents received ten more because of his faithfulness, then I'll get a lot more goodies in heaven if I'm more faithful. If the servant who was faithful in managing a few things was rewarded by his master giving him rulership over many things, then I'll be a great ruler in heaven if I'm faithful here and now."

This simple principle is expected at our jobs here on earth: "If I do a good, honest job, then I expect to be rewarded with more salary and advancement." And I support that kind of work ethic. No one likes to see people rewarded with advancement for reasons other than honest, productive labor. We're discouraged and angry when a coworker advances because of their dishonesty, manipulation, undermining of their coworkers, or even sexual favors. *It's just not right!*

Thus, it seems natural to expect that God would function in the same manner: reap what you sow. Therefore, an honest, disciplined Christian life is rewarded by heavenly advancement of both authority and goodies.

So my troubling question once again is, "Would you live such a self-sacrificing life IF there were no heavenly perks, just an entrance ticket to pass through heaven's gates?" Be honest.

It's a question that tugs at your motivations. Would you relax a bit from the striving if the reward is the same either way? If you believe your salvation is secure, then why would you live a disciplined, self-sacrificing life? To earn heavenly rewards?

Giving to Get

Actually, this traditional rewards concept is a "give-to-get" motivation. If at this point you're feeling a bit uncomfortable, please follow along as I probe a bit further into the dark forest with a promise to emerge into the light. A "give-to-get" philosophy is simple: give something to get something more valuable. It's a life principle played out over and over. We give time and money to earn a bachelor, masters or doctoral degree, believing the knowledge, the career and financial rewards will outweigh our investment. Lovers are willing to unselfishly give of themselves to their marital partner believing that they'll get even more in return.

This is good. So we naturally apply that same principle to our religion and find biblical texts that seem supportive. Matthew 19:29: "And every one that hath forsaken houses, or brethren, or sisters, or father, or mother, or wife, or children, or lands, for my name's sake, shall receive a hundredfold, and shall inherit everlasting life." (KJV)

So you ask, "Notice that the text says we will receive "a hundredfold" *and* "inherit everlasting life." Isn't this implying that our rewards are in addition to our ticket through the pearly gates?" My answer: "Yes it does, BUT what are these rewards? Are they actually rulership positions and better housing in heaven—or something else?" Hold that question.

Let me express one more concern for the traditional "give-to-get" philosophy in religion. Many preachers express this philosophy in different words, such as "plant the seed of faith if you wish to receive your heart's desire, be it health, wealth or love." Most of the time that "planting the seed of faith" means "bring your financial seed offerings forward and place them in the preacher's receptacles." In other words, give your money to my ministry IF you want to be blessed with healing, wealth or love.[25]

Recent worst case examples of this "give-to-get" seed offerings philosophy have been televangelists Robert Tilton, W.V. Grant, Paul Crouch (Trinity Broadcasting Network), Larry Lea, and Benny Hinn. Even the powerful and provocative preacher T.D. Jakes has not escaped the lure of this "give-to-get" virus. His 2014 sermon *Don't Waste the Water* is based on the concept that the floodgates of heaven's blessings are ready to open and flow into your life if you have the faith to plant the seed in the ground.

---

[25] Some refer to this teaching as "Prosperity Theology" wherein God has unconditionally set aside for you wealth, health and love. Your reception of such is simply an act of faith – such as bringing a large offering – which will open the "flood gates of heaven" resulting in a flood of all the goodies your heart could wish for.

Pastor Jake's words are:

> How can we have harvest unless we put seed in the ground... I want everyone in here who has the faith to do it, to sow your best seed here tonight. Get your seed into the ground for your company, for your business, for your idea, for your property, for that degree you're trying to finish. I want you to get your seed into the ground so it can get wet from the floodgates of heaven.

This appeal is followed by the choir singing *"Open the floodgates of heaven; let it flow,"* during which hundreds of congregants pushed to the front of the auditorium to drop their offering envelopes over the rail onto the preaching platform.

If you Google their worship services, you will eventually hear the same basic pitch. Some of these preachers may have used their huge offerings to truly bless the orphans and needy but usually we discover that they exploited their followers in order to live a lush, opulent lifestyle. And many of them will defend their lavish lifestyle as an example of what their faithful believers might enjoy both here and in the hereafter IF they were to be as faithful. No wonder then that so many critics believe that Christianity is a self-centered religion that exploits the ignorant for personal gain.

Lest I be misunderstood on this point, the Bible does teach a "reap what you sow" philosophy and God does promise to bring you blessings if you are faithful stewards of His gifts. But He has no selfish interest in our offerings to elevate His lifestyle and put another Mercedes Benz in His garage. (After all, He owns it all anyway.) Also, the Bible never says we'll get rich, healthy, and become popular and powerful if we drop more money in the offering plate. Instead, the Bible promises blessings—undefined and at the Lord's discretion. God's appointed blessing might be peace, joy, unselfish character development and, on rare occasion, a financial blessing.

With these sad examples of the "give-to-get" philosophy these same doubters then hear more honest preachers teaching: "No, your reward may not be here, but if you're faithful you will receive a reward even greater in heaven." What is implied by that promise? Answer: Heavenly rewards will be personal honor and power coupled with nicer homes and other goodies: things you don't have here... at least not enough to your liking. Like the old gospel song proclaims:

I'm satisfied with just a cottage below;
A little silver and a little gold.
But in that city where the ransomed will shine;
I want a gold one that's silver lined.

Did Jesus die *because* the Father promised to elevate Him to a throne of greater honor and power? No!

Let's face it, that appeals to the same selfish nature. The Bible calls that selfish nature within us a sinful character. It is NOT an example of the character of Jesus who forsook all the goodies of heaven in order to save an unworthy person such as you or me. The Bible says that Jesus *"for the joy that was set before him endured the cross."* Hebrews 12:2 (KJV)

What future "joy" motivated Jesus to make such a sacrifice? A "give-to-get" philosophy would say He gave much so that the Father would exalt Him, so that all would bow down and worship Him, the reward being more honor and power. But did Jesus do it for selfish reasons? Or simply because He "loved the world (meaning you and me) so much that He was not willing that any of us should perish"? John 3:16, 17. That second option sounds like the Jesus I love and serve.

Right now some of you are thinking about Philippians 2:3-11:

> In your relationships with one another, have the same mindset as Christ Jesus: Who, being the very nature God, did not consider equality with God something to be used to his own advantage; rather, he made himself nothing by taking the very nature of a servant, being made in human likeness. And being found in appearance as a man, he humbled himself by becoming obedient to death—even death on a cross!
>
> Therefore God exalted him to the highest place and gave him the name that is above every name, that at the name of Jesus every knee should bow in heaven and on earth and under the earth, and every tongue acknowledge that Jesus Christ is Lord, to the glory of God the Father.

So, it sounds like God the Father did reward Jesus' sacrifice by exalting Him to a place of honor and power. Then, isn't that an example of the reward of the saints?

Before making that leap of logic, think about this. Was Jesus' sacrifice a "give-to-get" gift? Did He do it for the glory, honor and power or did He do it because we are His children and He loves us SO much that He just HAD to sacrifice Himself, that He might be able to enjoy the fellowship of at least a few of us for eternity? We believe His motivation was that of sacrificial love.

But He will be honored, as the Son of God should be. Philippians 2:10 says that "every knee" will bow. Perhaps that means that, not just the saints but, every lost soul will someday bow and confess that Jesus' judgments (even for the damned) were just.

Was Jesus' Death a Give-to-Get Mission?

If Jesus was on a "give-to-get" mission with the hope that millions of saints would someday bow in worship before Him, why do we often say "Jesus would have died for the salvation of just one sinner"—you know, the one lost sheep? If true, then having just one rescued saint in heaven to bow before Jesus would have been a very poor gamble IF His motivation was to "give up a pawn in order to gain a kingdom." In other words, the adoration of only one saint bowing before Him would be a poor return on such a painful and risky sacrifice. *Unless* that one person were a son or daughter that He loved SO much that He couldn't restrain Himself. The Gospels are clear: Jesus' mission was 100% a sacrifice of love without thought of personal gain.

Then we would say that the Father's reward had no bearing on Jesus desire to sacrifice Himself. It was a perk that played no part in His motivation to give. The fact that His giving would open the way so that even a few of His human sons and daughters would accept and enjoy eternity with Him was motivation enough. In no way was He tempted by the selfish "give-to-get" bribe which implies: "If you want honor and power then you must give a seed faith offering... which, Jesus, in your case is your death on the cross."

In fact, look at that Hebrews 12:2 statement again: "Looking unto Jesus the author and finisher of our faith; who for the joy that was set before him endured the cross, despising the shame, *and* is set down at the right hand of the throne of God." (KJV)

What was the "joy that was set before him"? It was NOT the sitting down on the right hand of God because that is a textual afterthought. Notice the "*and* is set down." The "joy" part is not related to the "sitting on the throne" part. Jesus experienced the joy of his sacrifice—which was the vindication of His Father as being a just and loving God PLUS the salvation of many sinners—"and" sat at the right hand of God.

Here's a bold thought. Most world religions are based on a form of the "give-to-get" philosophy, i.e., if you take enough pilgrimages, spin enough prayer wheels, step across enough hot coals, lay on a bed of nails, give enough offerings, or become a martyr for Allah, then you will gain paradise where you will be appropriately rewarded. If you believe that the Christian's motivation for living a disciplined, sacrificial life is to gain heavenly rewards, then your religion is basically the same "give-to-get" religion as all the rest.

The primary difference then, between Christianity and other world religions, is that Christian salvation is cheap and free.

The Greatest Reward: Being Drawn Together, Heart-to-Heart

"So, don't you believe there is ANY distinction of rewards for the saints?" you may ask. Yes I DO believe in heavenly rewards. *But the only reward I can understand is the reward of being drawn closer together heart-to-heart, soul-to-soul to someone I respect and love that comes as the result of a "common experience of suffering and serving."*

Meaning what?

My dad was in Europe during World War II. He walked ashore at Omaha Beach in France just a shortly after the June 6, 1944, D-Day invasion. He followed our troops all the way into Germany. His outfit was constantly vulnerable to homesickness and death. Many believed that they would never see their family again. The bond he formed with those soldiers became so deep, so unique (some would say there's no bond like that formed with your buddy in a foxhole) that until his death at seventy-seven he faithfully attended reunions with his fellow survivors.

My mom later recited stories of how some of these veterans "worshiped my dad," their sergeant. This affection for

The Reward of Common Experience

each other never waned over the decades, a bond forged in the fires of a common experience—the hell of war.

That bond was a great "reward" for their military service. It was much more valuable than a medal or piece of paper acknowledging their faithful and honorable service. My mom went to the military reunions and came to love some of my dad's buddies, but she was never capable of the bond my dad had with them. His bond was formed "in the trenches."

Thus, I believe the greatest heavenly reward will that of enjoying for eternity the close bonding of our hearts with Jesus, based upon our common experience of suffering and serving. Those who have suffered and served the most will, naturally, have the closest bond with Jesus.

I believe that the saints who sing what John the Revelator calls the song of "Moses and the Lamb" are doing such because they have had a similar life of sacrifice and pain for the Kingdom. John describes them as having gone through great suffering: "those who had been victorious over the beast and its image and over the number of its name." Revelation 15:2-3

I tend to think that this is the same group described in chapter 14:3: "And they sang a new song before the throne and before the four living creatures and the elders. No one could learn the song except the 144,000 who had been redeemed from the earth."

With millions of years to learn a new tune, why can't all the saints learn this song?

Because it is a song that one can only know "in their heart and soul" by going through a common experience.

These saints had gone through a great tribulation which allowed them to better understand and appreciate the deep suffering that Jesus endured, both in His ministry and on the cross. Their hearts and souls are melted together, not because they accumulated holy deeds, but because they faced the fiery trials at a very deep and severe level. They trusted God to sustain them and remained faithful. Just like Jesus trusted His Father.

By the way, why is it called the song of "Moses and the Lamb"? Of course, Jesus (the "Lamb of God") faced trials that exceeded that of any human. But why Moses? Could it be for two reasons? First, Moses, like Jesus, was willing to lay his eternity on the line so that his people might be saved.[26] And, second, the experience of leading the "stiff necked" Israelites in the wilderness for forty years is probably the closest one can come to experiencing crucifixion at the hands of those one loves. Jesus and Moses have a "common experience" of suffering and serving which binds their hearts together in a manner that none can understand, except those saints who have gone through "great tribulation" here on earth.

Thus, it seems that both logically and biblically there ARE rewards in heaven. But these likely are not privileges, power, nor possessions that God bestows upon people who have lived a disciplined and holy life, although varying responsibilities and tasks may well be assigned to the saints. Instead, it is a bond of trust and love. Love acquired through extreme pain (a "fellowship of pain"), suffering, and faithfulness. Such will naturally unite their hearts into closer fellowship with Jesus throughout eternity.

When we sing the songs of praise around God's throne, all will feel a rapture of heart. But those who have faithfully endured the greatest testing and suffering will experience a reward, a thrill, and a fellowship that surpasses all the rest.[27]

---

[26] Exodus 32 records the Israelites molding and worshiping a golden calf at the foot of Mt. Sinai while Moses was in the mountain talking with God. God was so upset that he threatened to wipe out the whole camp. But in verses 31-32 we find Moses saying to the Lord, "Oh, what a terrible sin these people have committed. They have made gods of gold for themselves. But now, if you will only forgive their sin—but if not, erase my name from the record you have written!"

[27] Another common parallel many understand is the love for life that many folks have AFTER they have survived a near death experience. They see life, family and beauty with a greatly enhanced appreciation. They seldom

The Reward of Common Experience

THAT is the greatest of all rewards... and it cannot be earned. Only experienced.

Now, let's move from the rewards of the "yet to come" to those in the "here and now" that a whatEVER attitude promises.

---

can adequately explain the change but will say, "You'll never understand until you go through a similar experience."

Imagination Station #9

❄

What will it be like in heaven to see design and beauty in that which now looks like meaningless chaos? In the book "Fractals: The Patterns of Chaos" (1992) author John Briggs gives over 170 illustrations to explain the significance—and more importantly, the beauty—of fractals.

Fractals are unique patterns left behind by the unpredictable movements—the chaos—of the world at work. What to the naked eye appears as chaotic is, under more careful analysis, actually beautiful patterns. The branching patterns of trees, the veins in a hand, water twisting out of a running tap—all of these are fractals. Computer buffs have been able to trace the "chaotic" movement of rising smoke or rushing water. The computer printouts of these here-to-for believed to be chaotic and turbulent movements turn out to be the most intricate and beautiful designs.

Fractals permeate our lives, appearing in places as tiny as the surface of a virus and as majestic as the Grand Canyon. Perhaps the easiest fractal we're aware of is a snowflake. Together, snowflakes look like blobs to our normal vision, but under the microscope we see an unlimited variety of beautiful patterns.

Briggs notes that if we recognize the visual fractals then we would never again view things in quite the same way. It would revolutionize the way we see the world and our place with it. In heaven, those limitations will be removed, and we'll see all the beautiful patterns in what now appear to us as chaotic movement.

And while we're on the subject of sight, need we remind ourselves that our visual spectrum is SO limited? The visual spectrum also includes radio waves, microwaves, infrared

The Reward of Common Experience

waves, ultraviolet waves, X-ray waves and gamma rays. What will it be like to someday see all of the visual waves?

Also consider this: We're told that 99% of us have three cones in our eyes to detect color. But 1% of the population has four cones (called "tetrachromatic vision") and can see an estimated one hundred times more colors than the rest of us. One such person, Concetta Antico, is an artist who explains what she sees when looking at a leaf: "Around the edge I'll see orange or red or purple in the shadow; you might see dark green but I'll see violet, turquoise, blue... It's like a mosaic of color."

How many more colors will we be able to see in heaven when that which our "eye hath not seen" suddenly becomes visible?

Section IV:

The Whatever Factor Difference

Chapter 10:

Heaven Is For Disciples

"Therefore go and make disciples of all nations." Jesus

After forty-three years of pastoral ministry, I'm convinced that many Christians have the mistaken concept the saved can fall into either one of two groups and still make it to heaven:
1. "Children of God" who at one time accepted Jesus, come to church occasionally, volunteer when convenient, and have a WHATever attitude, meaning they follow all of God's commands when it doesn't interfere with their personal desires.
2. "Disciples" who take their faith seriously with a whatEVER attitude of obedience and service—the 20% in a congregation who passionately serve, care, obey, and sacrifice for the glory of God and His kingdom.

That's sad.

Even sadder is the fact that some preachers believe the same. For example, Dr. Charles Stanley, who writes: "Discipleship has nothing to do with whether you will go to heaven or not....

It is possible to be a child of God and never a disciple of Christ." *Handbook for Christian Living,* p. 505.

In theological discussions with my clerical peers, I have often raised my hand to say: "I disagree with you, but love you anyway." As I write now, my hand is raised. I have to disagree with Stanley, because I agree with Jesus.

You will never find in the Gospels any teaching of Jesus that portrays two types of saints bound for heaven:
1. Those who become devoted disciples: the whatEVER attitude.
2. Those who are merely believers: the WHATever attitude.

Nor does Jesus portray two types of heavenly neighborhoods: 1) the happy place, where all are praising God and, 2) the dark place, with weeping and gnashing of teeth. The only two groups that Jesus mentions are the sheep and goats, the faithful and the unfaithful, the saved and the lost. AND heaven is *everywhere* a place of light, joy and love.

All people are God's children, but not all will be in heaven. For this discussion let's equate the term *saint* as being synonymous with *disciple*.

Disciple vs. Believer

There is a great difference between a disciple and a believer. (Perhaps some will understand this better if I use the terms *disciple* and *volunteer*.) A believer/volunteer gets to set her own schedule. A volunteer calls his own shots. A volunteer comes and goes as she pleases. A volunteer can choose to just walk away when challenges arise. A volunteer can be a WHATever believer and obey only those commands of Jesus that don't interfere with his/her chosen lifestyle.

How about a disciple? Now there's a follower who stays with it through thick and thin—driven by a whatEVER attitude.

There are many metaphors that attempt to describe our relationship with Jesus. "Becoming a child of God" is a popular one. This is a bit ironic because every person by birth is a child of God whether they know and love Him or not. Many are children of God but don't know it. These await for one of God's followers to share the Good News; others are prodigals and don't WANT to be recognized as God's child. When a person is converted he is said to be reborn, a type of second birth to become a SAVED child of God welcomed back into the heavenly family.

Discipleship is also like getting married. I've never challenged a couple at the altar with a vow which says, "Do you promise to remain faithful and true to him as long as things go your way and the tough times don't last very long." No! Marriage is a lifelong vow... or at least it should be. It's a vow of mutual trust and discipleship. In the wedding analogy Jesus is the bridegroom and His disciples are His bride. Becoming a disciple of Jesus is a spiritual marriage. We promise to do whatEVER it takes to remain faithful and true to Jesus. Yes, we will falter and make mistakes, but we know that Jesus reads our hearts and never withholds forgiveness from the repentant disciple.

Every disciple of Jesus must listen when He says, "Deny yourself. Come, and follow me. Yes, there will be tests, tough times, disappointments, but take on the same attitude of submission that I had toward my Father and your rewards for faithfulness will be eternal."

Jesus never told us to go and make merely believers—he told us to go and make disciples. True? He doesn't call us to pitch in—he calls us to surrender all as we work together in His kingdom. In fact, Jesus' parting mandate to the apostles was: "Therefore go and make *disciples* of all nations, baptizing them in the name of the Father and of the Son and of the Holy Spirit, and teaching them to obey everything I have commanded you.

And surely I am with you always, to the very end of the age." Matthew 28: 18-20

Can you imagine Jesus saying: "Go and make disciples of a few and believers/volunteers of the rest. Teach the disciples to have a whatEVER attitude toward obeying everything I have commanded. To the believers with a WHATever attitude toward doing all that I have commanded, it will get them into heaven as long as they had a sincere conversion experience."

So, What IS a Disciple?

As we look at Jesus' life we see in Him two indisputable characteristics of being a radical, sold out disciple of His Father.[28]

Jesus turns to us and says, "As the Father has sent me, so I send you." He set the example which He expects His followers to emulate. **A disciple leaves things important to him or her to follow only Jesus.**

Jesus left heaven because he was a disciple of His Father. The Apostle Paul says that Jesus, even though He was equal with God the Father, didn't think twice about leaving heaven and choosing to become a servant, even unto death. Being a disciple ALWAYS means leaving cherished stuff in order to enjoy something eternally better. He told Nicodemus to leave his old thought patterns and be born again. He told the disciples that they must leave home, family, and job to follow him: "A teacher of the law came to [Jesus] and said, 'Teacher, I will follow you wherever you go.' Jesus replied, 'Foxes have dens and birds have nests, but the Son of Man has no place to lay his head.'" Matthew 8:18-20

And again, "He who loves father or mother more than Me is not worthy of Me. And he who loves son or daughter more than Me is not worthy of Me. And he who does not take

---

[28] I am grateful to Bill Hybels, pastor of Willow Creek Community Church, for first articulating for me these insights into what defines a disciple.

his cross and follow after Me is not worthy of Me." Matthew 10:37-38 (NKJV)

The sad reality of substituting volunteerism for discipleship is that a volunteer can participate without ever leaving anything. You can count on that person to help if they can fit it into their schedule, often built more around self-serving rather than kingdom interests. Many people even live under the delusion that they can have the blessings of Christ without living a sacrificial transformed life.

But Jesus made it unmistakably clear that "to leave behind" includes leaving the old life and being transformed into His likeness, as well as sacrificing relationships and possessions: "Therefore if any man be in Christ, he is a new creature: old things are passed away; behold, all things are become new." 2 Corinthians 5:17 (KJV)

Then Jesus raises the stakes by stressing what happens if we don't leave the old life and become transformed. He compares it to salt that has lost its savor: "Let me tell you why you are here. You're here to be salt-seasoning that brings out the God-flavors of this earth. If you lose your saltiness, how will people taste godliness? You've lost your usefulness and will end up in the garbage." Matthew 5:13 (MSG)

The garbage? Jesus is not referring to Stanley's dark neighborhood in heaven. Garbage means lost. Yes, we recycle garbage, but salt is not recycled. It becomes useless. Jesus is saying, "Either you become transformed disciples or you are useless to My kingdom."

Wes Roberts[29] writes: "Increasingly, the church is becoming marginalized. We're relegated to the fringes of our culture. We're rarely taken seriously. The vast majority of people in our society think the church is irrelevant.

---

[29] Wes Roberts is the author of *Support Your Local Pastor* and founder/CEO of Leadership Design Group/Life Enrichment, a worldwide ministry of mentoring, consulting and counseling to Christian leaders.

The Whatever Factor

Why? Maybe pollster George Barna has discovered the answer: "Of more than 70 moral behaviors we study, [Christian] believers are largely indistinguishable from non-believers in how they think and live."

The obvious conclusion is that too many people professing to be Christians are really not His disciples. They have never desired or have lost interest in positively living out the character of Jesus. OR their Christianity was simply something they added to their broken life which brought some adjustments in their lifestyle without embracing total surrender. Perhaps they *know* they accepted Jesus and are saved, but becoming transformed into the character of Jesus is optional.

Like the "seed that fell among the rocks" in Jesus' parable of the sower (Matthew 13), they eagerly and sincerely accept the gospel of Jesus and enjoy exciting changes in some areas of their life. But when the going gets rough—or when Jesus reveals that they must "leave" some cherished possessions or lifestyle behaviors and develop a whatEVER attitude toward all of His commands—they either give up or embrace a WHATever attitude toward discipleship. All the while claiming to be "saved."

They remain broken, self-centered people wearing buttons on their lapel stating, "I'm a Jesus follower" and a bumper sticker that reads "Christians aren't perfect; they're just forgiven." But sadly they have never grasped or desired to become fully surrendered and broken, reborn, and reshaped by Jesus into a living incarnation of Jesus.

Jesus said, "If I be lifted up, I will draw all people to myself." John 12:32

Well, look around. A lot of people are not being drawn to Jesus, which begs the question, "Are we effectively lifting Him up in our lives and lifestyles?" Barna, and his team of pollsters say, "NO." Not happening. The salt is not seasoning. Our culture has leached the flavor from the salt rather than the salt seasoning our culture. Translated means: **Most Christians still**

reflect more the attitudes and behavior of those who don't know Jesus than the thoughts, attitudes, and behavior of Jesus himself.

Maybe the Apostle John's straight forward manner better grabs our attention: "The man who says, 'I know him,' but does not do what he commands is a liar, and the truth is not in him. But if anyone obeys his word, God's love is truly made complete in him. This is how we know we are in him: Whoever claims to live in him must walk as Jesus did." 1 John 2:4-6

So What Is a Disciple?

"As Jesus was walking beside the Sea of Galilee, he saw two brothers, Simon called Peter and his brother Andrew. They were casting a net into the lake, for they were fishermen. 'Come, follow me,' Jesus said, 'and I will make you fishers of men.' At once they left their nets and followed him." Matthew 4:18-20

In this text we see two of the most predictable behaviors of a true disciple who has a "whatEVER-Jesus-asks-I-will-do" attitude. When Jesus asked Peter and Andrew to become His disciples, they chose to 1) **leave something (surrender, leave behind) something important to them:** their fishing career. Within but a few years, they learned that they needed to leave much, much more... including life itself. Both died as martyrs.

They also needed to 2) **do and become something very different:** fishers of men. That involved a total character transformation. And it wasn't until after their denial of Jesus followed by his resurrection, that they accepted their need for this most important character transformation.

You see, Jesus was looking for disciples who were so radically committed to Him that they would willingly sacrifice everything. At that point He could transform them so fully into His likeness that they would be able to turn the world upside down for His kingdom. And the New Testament reveals that, in their transformed lives, they lifted Jesus up so compellingly that their world WAS turned upside down.

Radical commitment ALWAYS involves first leaving something in order to do or become something new:
1. You've got to give up dating around when you say "I Do" at the wedding altar.
2. You've got to give up a lot of your independence when you have a baby.
3. You've got to give up whatEVER Jesus asks you to leave behind in order to become a new person in Jesus Christ.
4. You've got to give up the line "that's just the way I am" and replace it with "that's what Jesus wants me to become."

I remember visiting a young woman who claimed to be a Christian and an official member of my congregation, yet had been living unmarried for some time with the most recent of her boyfriends.

In the course of conversation I asked, "Is living together your understanding of Jesus' will for you?"

"Of course not."

"Well, if you are knowingly and continually choosing not to do His will, isn't that a form of hypocrisy? Isn't hypocrisy defined by persistently choosing an attitude or lifestyle that violates one's profession?"

"Well, you can take my name off the church books if that's what you want."

"That's NOT what I want. What I want for you is integrity." I continued, "It seems to me that your integrity requires you to make a choice. Do you want to bring your lifestyle into harmony with your Christian profession, or should you stop professing something you choose not to live. I pray you will choose to change your lifestyle to harmonize with your Christian profession and please know that I will commit myself to doing whatever possible to help you do that. However, if your sense of integrity causes you to forgo your Christian profession in order to continuing living your current lifestyle, please know that I am not here to condemn. In fact, I would love to be the first person you turn to whenever you need help."

Was that too strong? What would Jesus have said, *"You must deny yourself, take up your cross and follow me"*? Or, *"A person who says 'I know Jesus' but does not do what I command is a liar and the truth is not in her."* Disciples choose to do whatEVER.

Hey, do Christians make mistakes? Do we sometimes (many times!) willingly choose to think and act in a manner out of harmony with Jesus? Of course. But hypocrisy is not just a mistake. It's a willing and persistent choice to live my way, not God's way; to not deny myself and, thus, to not be a disciple of Jesus. Being a disciple is a brutally difficult, self-sacrificing, everything-surrendered-on-the-altar kind of choice. But Jesus promised that such a dedicated decision on our part will be repaid a hundredfold.

You remember the movie, *Castaway*? Tom Hanks plays a man who has been shipwrecked on a tropical island. After several months without any human contact or hope of rescue, he finally tries to make an escape. He builds a raft and grabs "Wilson" his best friend, who happens to be a smudged leather volleyball. They head out over the breakers and eventually make it to calm waters.

Hanks falls asleep, and when he wakes up, Wilson is gone. He frantically calls out and notices that Wilson has broken loose and is bobbing up and down in the open ocean a few hundred feet from the raft. Diving into the sea with the panic of a parent who sees his child on the other side of the train tracks, Tom swims with all his might to save his friend.

Then, there is this excruciatingly defining moment: Hanks reaches out desperately with one hand for the drifting Wilson, with his other hand he is holding the rope that is connected to his raft. He's got to make a choice. The currents are slowly pulling Wilson away from him and the raft. He wants Wilson to stay with him more than anything, but he realizes that if he chooses Wilson over the raft, he gives up any hope of survival and rescue.

In the end Hanks is left weeping prostrate on the raft over the trauma of being caught between two things that are both important. He lets go of Wilson—later to be found asleep on his dilapidated raft by a rescuer.

To follow Jesus as His disciple we can't hang on to everything. We have to pick what to take, what is absolutely necessary according to Jesus and leave behind many things that have been important to us. What up to now has provided comfort may henceforth become a hindrance to where we want to go: to heaven.

In 1 Corinthians 6:9-11 Paul is talking to believers, people who call themselves Christ followers. Now Paul is challenging them to make some radical decisions regarding their journey to God's kingdom: "Don't you realize that this is not the way to live?... Those who use and abuse each other, use and abuse sex, use and abuse the earth and everything in it, don't qualify as citizens in God's kingdom." (MSG)

Indeed, we're all broken in some way... many ways. But strength never grows from brokenness unless we're willing to move in God's direction of healing. First step is to choose to let go of something. Next step, obey him... follow him... take a step in his direction. Then, allow Him to transform our mind.

Becoming a disciple is a journey, a leaving the old behind and becoming that new person, thinking new ways, obeying and doing life like Jesus.

My primary preaching focus during my pastoral ministry was on the radical, mind-blowing, inclusive love of God toward us, His undeserving children. But I sometimes worried that I left some worshipers with the impression that discipleship is optional, that because Jesus is very fond of broken, sinful people it's not important to make radical lifestyle and attitude changes.

In my sincere attempt to make church a safe place of loving acceptance[30] I may have allowed some to think that that the goal was inclusive acceptance without change.

Jesus calls all of us to radical love, radical acceptance, radical change, and radical commitment to be a new person. I simply believe that people are more willing to embrace and own their brokenness in a safe nonjudgmental environment. But embracing our brokenness is not our destination; it's only a necessary step toward our destination: becoming new, radically changed disciples of Jesus—so changed that our friends, our family and our community will believe Jesus is real as they see radical changes in us!

Jesus said, "They will KNOW because they SEE." (John 13:35) Yep, seeing IS believing.

Several years ago, government agricultural agents often tried to introduce to farmers new technologies, seeds (unfortunately, many were the GMO variety) and fertilizers that they claimed promised increased yields. Often the farmers resisted; they just didn't trust those government yahoos and their "new-fangled" ideas.

So the agents simply selected a strip of public land, usually along a major roadway, as a demonstration plot where their new farming methods, seed, and fertilizers were used to raise a crop. I remember seeing these little strips along the highway with a sign that identified what type of seed that was being demonstrated.

Throughout the summer the farmers remained skeptical as the crops grew. But their opinions usually changed in the fall when the demonstration crops performed better than their crops. It was clear to anyone who looked that the new crops were greener, taller, more productive than the old. And by the next

---

[30] The church should be the *"The Safest Place on Earth"* as Henry Cribb entitled his book.

year, many of the farmers were using the new technology, seed, or fertilizer—as if it were their own idea!

The church is, among other things, God's demonstration plot to the world. The local church is God's demonstration to that community as to whether there CAN be a faith community that embraces broken people without judging, while also helping these broken people become transformed into disciples, patterning their lives after Jesus.

So, let me be personal. If Jesus were to walk into your room and ask you to leave something, to deny yourself and become a radically committed disciple, a living and personal demonstration of a life transformed by His love, what might He ask you to leave behind? An addiction, a relationship, attitude, unforgiving spirit toward a certain person, a "I love you as long as it's my way" attitude, a sexual perversion, pornography, gossip, lying, manipulating spirit, your unwillingness to financially downsize your life for his kingdom?

Are you willing to leave all to become His disciple? Imagine yourself saying, "Yes, Lord, it's yours. I'm too weak to give it to You, but I give You permission to take it away. I WANT to be a disciple who fully incarnates your character and spirit."

Being a fully devoted disciple of Jesus and not just an "on again/off again" believer or volunteer.

It means that everything is affected. It can be unsettling... sometimes frightening. Change usually is, if it involves something dear and secure to you.

One of the most often repeated phrases in the Bible is God saying, "Trust me and do not be afraid." He usually said that when He was asking someone to surrender and change his way of thinking so that God's will could be fulfilled. In the next chapter we'll see just how personal this change must be.

Is your life defined by a WHATever attitude or (like Paul) a surrendered mind purposes "WhatEVER I eat or whatEVER I drink or whatEVER I do, I will do to the glory of God"?

Refusing to embrace this attitude of total commitment while calling oneself a disciple is unthinkable. Because true disciples are not merely loyal and obedient, they are primarily *lovers* who find their greatest joy in loving God supremely and serving their neighbors with the incarnate hands and fee of Jesus.

Imagination Station #10

Just as some visual fractals can only be seen with the correct measuring instruments, so also it's credible to believe in audible fractals: organized, harmonious, beautiful "music" emanating from what now sounds to us like the roar of a waterfall and the whoosh of wind in the trees and grass.

One writer who, like John the Revelator, claimed to have seen heaven in vision writes: "I saw a field of tall grass, most glorious to behold; it was living green and had a reflection of silver and gold, as it waved proudly to the glory of King Jesus."

In another place she notes that even the trees and waterfalls sang praise to their Creator. This is not meant to suggest that heaven is a pantheistic utopia where trees have spirits nor a place where, like in the movie "Avatar," all nature is mysteriously linked in some subconscious way to one controlling spirit power. Rather it suggests that God created all things to move and function in a manner perceived by our senses as giving glory to their Maker.

Also, humans hear only a small portion of the sound spectrum. What will it be like to hear ten or a hundredfold more sound frequencies? With our awesomely increased ability to hear the whole sound spectrum, there will be musical sounds and harmonies never before heard. A musician's paradise!

When our ears are opened to the full audible range to hear what "ear hath not heard," we will hear music from places where currently we hear nothing. We talk of the "silence of space," but now we know that space is NOT silent. The special instruments on the Voyager and other spacecraft have now recorded electromagnetic vibration sounds (video clips of such are on YouTube.com). The sounds ebb and flow, up and down.

What if with our heavenly hearing we discovered that these electromagnetic sounds are harmonious and organized into beautiful music? Maybe every galaxy has its own unique songbook of praise to God.

Chapter 11:

Heaven Is For Lovers

"Well done. I'm so proud of you. Come and enjoy the kingdom I've prepared for you." God

At his 50th wedding anniversary the husband was asked, "So what is the secret to your long marriage? Didn't you ever have disagreements or arguments?"

"Oh, yes, a lot of them. But early in our marriage we agreed that she could say most anything she wanted, if after that I could go outside for a walk. So the secret to our long marriage is that I have lived primarily as an outdoors man."

How important is it for you to win an argument? To get the final word, to get your way? What do you do when people disagree with you? Do you usually get it *your* way? Does it frustrate you when you don't?

We have a zoo at our house, but it used to be worse. We have this African Gray parrot named Ty. I call her "Silly Bird." She weighs only one pound, but acts like she owns the house. Then, a few years ago, we brought in a friend's African Gray to keep while they were on vacation. We put their cages close together, thinking that Silly Bird would be thankful for companionship.

Silly Bird hated that other parrot. When they were out of their cages our bird ran toward the other one trying to intimidate it and would pull out the other bird's feathers (literally) if we didn't stop her.

Once my sister-in-law went on vacation for a month and dropped off her two love birds. Silly Bird looked down on them in their small cage as if to say, "You're lucky there are bars between us, you chirpy little imps."

Then we had this cat, named "Pooh" after Pooh Bear. If Silly Bird was out of her cage, Pooh learned to sleep with one eye open because the bird would sneak up from behind and bite his tail. All of these aggressive antics just to prove to herself that she—a one-pound parrot!—was at the top of the pecking order. (Pun intended.)

If you put ten chickens in a cage, it wouldn't take but a few hours for the pecking order to be established. All of them would learn who was number one and ruled the roost.

The pecking order is not just among animals. You find it on an elementary school playground or in a university faculty lounge, among business people, in churches, among pastors, in marriages and families. There is a poorly disguised drive in humans to feel power over others, or at the least, to have it our way.

Boxer Mohammed Ali in his egotistical heyday (before Parkinsons disease brought him down), was best known for his shout, "I am the greatest!" One day he was taking a commercial flight and the attendant asked him to fasten his seat belt. "Superman don't need no seat belt."

"Well," the attendant replied, "if you were Superman you wouldn't need this airplane."

Few of us are as obvious about wanting to be honored as number one, but that form of arrogant pride is as common in our hearts as the blood it pumps. In fact, it is at the very core of our sin problem, starting in heaven with Lucifer when he said,

"I want to be number one."[31] It was used as the temptation in the Garden of Eden when Lucifer (now known as Satan) tempted Adam with the idea, "You can be number one, just like a god if you eat the fruit."[32] It has become the very bedrock of human cultures. That's why I've said in many sermons, "All cultures are flawed, so don't just say 'that's the way we do it.'"

Students of human behavior say that it's neither the lure of money nor the lure of pleasure nor the lust for sex that is the greatest human desire. Rather, the pursuit of power.

This pursuit takes many forms. It might be by force of arms and wars or by a wife giving the other the silent treatment and withholding sex or by a husband physically abusing his spouse. It might be by bullying or manipulating by financial control. It might be legal or illegal. It is rampant in the labor unions, in corporate board rooms, in politics, in families, and even in church organizations.

Jesus had an unmistakable opinion about this. So did other Spirit-inspired Scriptures:

> For those who exalt themselves will be humbled, and those who humble themselves will be exalted. Matthew 23:12

> The eyes of the arrogant will be humbled and human pride brought low; the LORD alone will be exalted in that day. Isaiah 2:11

> To fear the LORD is to hate evil; I hate pride and arrogance, evil behavior and perverse speech. Proverbs 8:13

---

[31] Isaiah 14:12-15.

[32] Genesis 3.

> Where there is strife, there is pride, but wisdom is found in those who take advice. Proverbs 13:10

Ponder this: "Where there is strife, there is pride." The sad thing about power is that one day we humans can put our arm around someone and say, "Let's pray together"—and the next day, because that person may be a threat to our job, our promotion, our finances or status or comfort, we run them down with gossip. In essence we are saying, "I love you as long as I can be number one," or "I love you as long as I get my way."

The disciples were like this, always in strife over who should be promoted to number one. Jesus ran into a whole culture of pride with the religious leaders.

Bill Hybels, in his book *Descending into Greatness*, writes:

> Jesus Christ hated the Pecking Order. In fact, He spent His entire ministry ripping at its foundations. He seized every opportunity to turn the Pecking Order upside down and inside out. Those who reached the top—the religious leaders of Israel—He often scorched with His words. He called them hypocrites, whitewashed tombs, snakes. He accused them of robbing widows, being filled with dead men's bones, and in so many words, worshiping themselves... [T]he religious leaders were, perhaps, the most important, powerful, and respected people in Israel—the VUPs—worthy, they believed, of great honor. Yet Jesus scorned them. He spurned the Pecking Order.[33]

---

[33] Bill Hybels, *Descending into Greatness*, Zondervan Publishing House, 1993, pg. 120.

The opposite of arrogant pride is humility. "When pride comes, then comes disgrace, but with humility comes wisdom." Proverbs 11:2

The dictionary defines *humility* as modesty, lacking pretense, not believing that you are superior to others. You can be proud of your achievements without being arrogantly proud. Someone once said, "Humility is not clothing ourselves in an attitude of self-abasement or self-denigration. Humility is all about maintaining our pride about who we are, about our achievements, about our worth – but without arrogance."

To have humility means that we don't have to have the last word, we don't have to be number one to feel valued. From where does this humility come? Well, you may be fortunate enough to have been taught such or have seen it exemplified in a parent or friend. But God is the source of all genuine humility.

Notice carefully the humility of Jesus, as noted in Philippians 2:3-8:

> Do nothing out of selfish ambition or vain conceit. Rather, in humility value others above yourselves, not looking to your own interests but each of you to the interests of the others. In your relationships with one another, have the same attitude of mind Christ Jesus had: Who, being in very nature God, did not consider equality with God something to be used to his own advantage; rather, he made himself nothing by taking the very nature of a servant, being made in human likeness. And being found in appearance as a human being, he humbled himself by becoming obedient to death—even death on a cross!

The phrase: *"Who, being in very nature God... made himself nothing by taking the very nature of a servant"* implies that, although He was in an exalted position as God, He chose to humble himself by coming to earth and dying. The first impression is, "Wow, Jesus humbling Himself like that is very much out of character, very unusual for God." But is it?

Another meaning of that Greek word which is translated "being in the very nature of God" is the word "because." Correctly translated, it would read, "Precisely *because* He was in the very nature of God... He made Himself nothing by taking the very nature of a servant."

In other words, humbling himself and serving was not something foreign to His Godness. Rather, it was *because* He is God, *because* He is love, it was the most natural thing in the universe for Him to choose to humble Himself to serve us. That's exactly what a Spirit-filled heart does.

And friends, that's what happens to us when we have God's heart with a whatEVER attitude. We stop trying to force our will on others, boasting, playing the game of I'm-better-than-you." And we stop trying to have the last word.

"Maybe you're right."

One of the phrases we begin to say more often when our heart reflects the character of Jesus is, "Maybe you're right." Try it. As the Proverb says: "Where there is strife, there is pride, but wisdom is found in those who take advice." Proverbs 13:10

One night a couple's argument degenerated into a childish, "You're wrong, I'm right" interchange. Finally, she said, "Okay, this is going no place. Let's just take a breath and step back. Now, if I admit that I might be wrong, would you be willing to say that I might be right?"

He thought for a moment and said, "Okay, you go first."

"All right, it is possible that I might be wrong,"

To which he blurted, "You're absolutely right!"

Now there was a man about to enjoy some more outdoor time.

Stop Trying to Prove Your Worth

A second thing that happens when our heart reflects Jesus with a whatEVER attitude is that we stop trying to prove our worth. When people don't feel valued at work, they often gossip or run others down. When people don't feel valued among their friends, they try to boast about their achievements, their dating experiences, their cars, their intelligence, their jewelry, etc,

But if you are secure in who you are and know your intrinsic value to your Heavenly Father, then you don't have to strive for power or control or attention in order to validate your worth. All you have to do is look up and say, "I'm a child of the King."

Listen carefully to God's description of you: "For those who are led by the Spirit of God are the children of God. The Spirit you received does not make you slaves, so that you live in fear again; rather, the Spirit you received brought about your adoption to sonship." Romans 8:14-15

Wow! How differently would we think or act or talk if every moment of the day we were fully conscious that we are a son or daughter of God? That we are loved beyond anything that is valued in this world?

Becoming Satisfied in Serving without Craving Recognition

A third thing that happens when our whatEVER heart reflects that of Jesus is that receiving recognition is appreciated, but no longer a craving. Someone once asked a church consultant, "How do you know if someone needs some words of appreciation?" Answer: "If they are breathing."

You know, that's true. I so often forget to reach out and thank people. It's gratifying to know that one's contribution is appreciated and makes a difference. But, when we are secure in Jesus and know our value in Him, you and I find ourselves craving less and less public recognition and we loosen our grip on getting it our way. We don't need monuments; we don't need buildings named after us.

During one sermon I challenged folks in my congregation (many of whom were corporate leaders and/or wealthy contributors) to actively dissuade any organization from naming a building after them—until after their death, if then. The temptation for pride is too risky. That's why Jesus said:

> Be careful not to practice your righteousness in front of others to be seen by them. If you do, you will have no reward from your Father in heaven. So when you give to the needy, do not announce it with trumpets, as the hypocrites do in the synagogues and on the streets, to be honored by others. Truly I tell you, they have received their reward in full. But when you give to the needy, do not let your left hand know what your right hand is doing, so that your giving may be in secret. Then your Father, who sees what is done in secret, will reward you. Matthew 6:1-4

As our heart becomes more like Jesus' heart, we serve more like He served. He was willing to serve even to the death of the cross for the joy that lay beyond. Not for human praise, which is so fickle and temporary, but for the praise of His Father in heaven.

I believe that is what Jesus meant on resurrection Sunday when he said to Mary Magdalene at the tomb, "Don't hold on to me for I have not yet ascended to my Father." He wanted to approach His Father and say, "I have finished my mission. The victory is won." And He wanted to hear His Father's words of affirmation and appreciation, "Well done, My Son." Human praise and worship was always secondary to the praise of His Father.

And you know, someday we will hear the same, "Well done, my son, my daughter. Come inherit the kingdom prepared for you."

A college quarterback was asked how he remained focused when tens of thousands of spectators in the stadium were shouting and the hype was high and the TV cameras were rolling. He calmly replied, "Because I don't play to the crowds. I know my coach is watching, and I play the game only to him. He's the one who really knows if I'm playing well."

If God were to put the epitaph on your life, what would it be?
1. "He thought he was better than most."
2. "She did it her way."
3. "Well done, good and faithful servant.

Years ago when I read Max Lucado's book *The Applause of God*,[34] it triggered a memory.

One summer Saturday afternoon in 1991 in New England, my oldest teenage son and I were wondering what to do. I said, "I just read that Desert Storm troops are returning from the Gulf and landing at the Westover Air Force base near Springfield, Massachusetts. The public is invited." It was only an hour or so away, so we went.

Upon arriving we stepped into a cavernous airplane hangar. The large door was closed but next to it was the people-size door. From that small door was rolled out a red carpet that extended about half way across the hangar and emptied into a roped off area where there was an abundance of goodies that the soldiers could feast upon. "Comfort" food that may have been sparse in the desert, like hot dogs, Coke, ice cream and other fat and sugar laden yummies.

The red carpet was lined on both sides with stanchions and more rope. On each side of the carpet were hundreds of appreciative and eager local folks. The unspoken yet commonly

---

[34] Max Lucado, *The Applause of Heaven*, Nelson, Thomas, Inc. 1996.

shared attitude was, "Earlier troops were called 'baby murderers' and spat upon when they returned from Viet Nam. We're here to make sure that our Desert Storm troopers get a proper welcome."

As we mingled, news spread that the planes were arriving about every forty-five minutes and that this was the first American soil they would touch. The soldiers would disembark, stretch their limbs, eat some goodies, and then fly on to their respective bases.

"The next plane is now touching down," echoed the voice in the loudspeaker. "The soldiers will be sent to the adjoining hangar where they will leave their weapons. Then they'll come to this hangar for some food. They do not know that a welcoming party is awaiting them."

Oh, cool. That made the excitement even more palatable. This was to be a SURPRISE PARTY!

Everyone stopped talking and shuffling. The hangar was quiet. All eyes focused on that single door at the end of the red carpet. Finally, it swung open and in walked the first trooper— completely outfitted as though he had just left the desert with backpack, camouflage uniform and helmet.

The hangar exploded into cheering, clapping, yelling, and whistling. I can whistle really loud, but I couldn't even hear myself for the echoing and reverberating cacophony of noise. The response of each soldier was similar. At first they jerked their head up with a "What's going on here?" expression. Then their faces broke out into gracious smiles. They nodded and waved in an attempt to say, "Thank you."

Then a couple elementary-aged girls approached them and gave them clear plastic bags of toiletries and other little necessaries that they had probably missed in the desert. The children hugged them politely and ushered them down the red carpet to the eating area. It was all very moving and sweet.

But then the burly sergeant swaggered in. Tall, broad-shouldered, confident, cool. He smiled and waved his appreciation to the applauding crowd. He was a man in control: the iconic soldier. He leaned down and thanked the girls for their gifts and their hug. Then he strode on down the carpet until...

Leaning against the rope in an attempt to be seen and to be as close to the returning soldiers as possible was a withered-looking hundred-pound Viet Nam veteran in his jungle fatigues. The jungle green uniform was clean, the soft crumply cap clung to his head... and his hands clutched the crutches. The destructive effects of drugs, war, and pain had taken their obvious toll. But there he stood, as straight as possible.

The burly sergeant saw him out of the corner of his eye. He turned and walked up to the Viet Nam vet, stopping only inches from his face. He set his plastic bag down, took his backpack off and placed it on the carpet, then stood at attention face-to-face, eye-to-eye with the vet (so to speak since there was a foot height difference).

Amidst the deafening noise of the crowd, an unspoken message was conveyed between these two veterans. The Viet Nam vet looking up and seeming to say, "I did whatEVER it took to get here and make sure you get the welcome I never received. Welcome home, soldier. We're so proud of you."

The aged vet, standing as erect as his frail body would allow, snapped and held a salute. The Desert Storm sergeant snapped a salute in return as if to say, "Brother, I got the message and your welcome will mean more to me than any I'll ever receive."

Then the big soldier dropped his salute, leaned in and gave the little vet a huge bear hug. That was a "welcome home" I will never forget.

Now, imagine Jesus escorting you through the pearly gates down the golden boulevard that leads to the throne of God the Father. The wide street is lined with bleachers with millions of heavenly angels all sitting in silence. In fact, there is no sound at all, just you and Jesus walking toward the throne.

As you near the Almighty, He slowly stands and his eyes that burn like fire yet are brimming with love looking at you, or

The Whatever Factor

more accurately look right through you. You cannot approach such majesty, yet Jesus leans over and whispers "It's okay. He's here to welcome you home."

Then the silence is broken by the mighty voice of the Father, like that of a hundred waterfalls and the sound of many thunders. "Well done. I am so proud of you."

In a measured fashion the Father slips his hands out from within His garments and begins to clap. Slowly at first but faster and with greater enthusiasm. The angels, like a mighty wave of thunder, join the applause with shouts and cheers. Soon, all heaven is rocking and rolling with the raucous noise of celebration.

You look with a question in your eye toward Jesus. He responds not with words but in a message you feel in your soul, "Yes, the applause is for you."

Can you imagine yourself relishing such an awesome moment? How could you envision such an awesome scene without your pulse quickening as you imagine yourself actually experiencing it? I can't wait for that moment and—think of this—Jesus can't wait to surprise us with this and even more.

This is Jesus' promise to every disciple who is learning to love like He loves. It will be the greatest reward for those whose life is defined by "whatEVER I eat or drink or whatEVER I do, I'll do it all for the glory of God."

Jesus—and all the biblical writers—want you to BE there. That's why they caution us to be on watch and search our hearts, lest we deceive ourselves that we are heaven-bound when, in reality, we're heading down the path that leads to destruction. That is the subject of our next chapter.

Imagination Station #11

Phil Plait, an astronomer who studies photos taken by the Hubble telescope, recently wrote: "In my time on Hubble we'd routinely see background galaxies that were well over a billion light years away. Routinely. Mind you, each of these background objects is itself an entire galaxy, containing tens or hundreds of billion of stars, perhaps as big, rich, and diverse as our own Milky Way."

*He continues: "And yet the Universe is deeper even than that. It stretches on and on... and while it's finite — it has an actual size — in practical terms it's infinite. Why? Because it's expanding. If you could somehow hitch a ride on a photon, the fastest thing in the cosmos (A photon in a vacuum travels at 300,000 kilometers per second), you'd still never reach the edge of the Universe even if it had one. That's because the edge would be receding away from you faster than you could reach it. You'd forever be playing catch-up. Literally, **forever**.*

In 2018 NASA expects to launch the next generation telescope, the James Webb. Webb will have a 6.5 meter diameter primary mirror compared to Hubble's smaller 2.4 meters in diameter, giving Webb around 7 times more collecting area!

A recent German super-computer simulation estimates that there may be as high as 500 billion galaxies, with many older than the Milky Way. How will this number increase when the Webb telescope snoops even deeper into space?

With all of eternity to explore and billions of galaxies awaiting our discovery, can you imagine activities and adventures more interesting in heaven than riding on a lion?

Chapter 12:

How Far Is Heaven?

"There is a generation that are pure in their own eyes, and yet is not washed from their filthiness." Proverbs 30:12 (ASV)

Are you aware that the Bible speaks of three heavens? The first is for those who believe in a bar code religion—the "once saved always saved," who accepted Jesus once in their life but lived mostly ungodly lives thereafter. Their heaven is a dark place with people who definitely believe in God and go to church occasionally and have a "do what the Bible teaches if it is convenient" approach to life. They don't become real disciples and they generally have a "WHATever" attitude toward lifestyle change.

The second heaven is for Pharisees and legalists who work very hard to get to heaven. They go to church three times a week, fast and give double tithes, and have check-in stations on the street corners and in their homes to record how many good deeds they have done that day. They have a "you've-never-done-enough" attitude. Their "black and white" heaven is a rather stiff, judgmental place.

How Far Is Heaven?

The third heaven is for broken people, sinners who are so sick and tired of being slaves to sin that they not only accept Jesus' forgiveness but have a passion for really knowing Him and experiencing His loving character recreated in their hearts. They have a "whatEVER God wants for me... *that* is what I want for myself" attitude. The atmosphere in their heaven can best be described as one pulse beat of love and light that permeates the whole universe.

Which heaven might be your destination?

Of course, I'm joking. But this is a good review of the three theories of salvation that we have studied. Yes, there are three heavens mentioned in Scripture, but they are described much differently:

The first heaven is where the birds fly in the air we breathe. Deuteronomy 28:12: "The Lord will open the heavens, the storehouse of his bounty, to send rain on your land in season and to bless all the work of your hands."

The second heaven is the starry heavens. Psalm 19:4, 6 (NRSV): "In the heavens he has pitched a tent for the sun.... It rises at one end of the heavens and makes its circuit to the other."

The third heaven is where Jesus said he was going to prepare us a place to live. Matthew 5:16: "In the same way, let your light shine before men, that they may see your good deeds and praise your Father in heaven."

So how far is heaven? Depends on which heaven you're talking about. But more important, how far is God? The Bible says His throne and dwelling place is in the third heaven, way beyond the starry second heaven and even farther above our head than the clouds. Since God's dwelling place is in the third heaven, humans sometimes feel that He's so far away that He's unreachable and uninterested.

But then we find the beautiful Gospel story that tells us of the babe of Bethlehem who came to dwell, not in the third heaven, not in the second heaven of the stars, but in our first heaven to breathe our air and cough on our dust. Emmanuel: not God up there, but "God with us."

WHY? Most pagan gods don't bother about getting close to their people. Instead, they demand that their people try to get close to them—with sacrifices, pilgrimages and offerings. (That is one of the two key differences between Christianity and most other world religions.[35]) But God the Father allowed His son Jesus to live among us because He loves us and has a passionate desire to have us know and love Him. He knows the destructive power of sin more than we do and desperately desires to unshackle us from its slavery. He wants us to respond with a growing passion to know and love Him so much that our strongest desire is to be like Him and live with Him forever... in all three heavens.

I have sometimes wrestled with what it means to be saved and who really will be in heaven. I have noted in Scripture that just working hard to earn salvation couldn't be true, or Paul would not have said, "For it is by grace you have been saved, through faith—and this is not from yourselves, it is the gift of God—not by works, so that no one can boast." Ephesians 2:8-9

I am convinced that access to heaven is based on a relationship with Jesus, not an entrance exam of good deeds nor merely by a bar code event of accepting Jesus. Jesus said: "Now this is eternal life: that they *know* you, the only true God, and Jesus Christ." John 17:3 In an earlier chapter I indicated that the word "know" often refers to an intimate relationship or love. In this verse (and others) we could replace "know" with "love" as in, "This is eternal life: that they *love* you, the only true God and Jesus Christ."

---

[35] The second difference is best described by rock singer Bono: "Christianity is the only religion that interrupts the karma cycle." Meaning? Christianity is the only religion where we don't suffer the appropriate fate for our sin. The wages of sin is death, but that karma cycle was interrupted when Jesus died FOR us. He broke the karma cycle by His grace.

Jesus also indicated that simply accepting Him and claiming to be a follower does not guarantee our ticket to heaven either: "Not everyone who says to me, 'Lord, Lord,' will enter the kingdom of heaven, but only those who do the will of my Father who is in heaven. Many will say to me on that day, 'Lord, Lord, did we not prophesy in your name and in your name drive out demons and in your name perform many miracles?' Then I will tell them plainly, 'I never knew you. Away from me, you evildoers!'" Matthew 7:21-23

I shared that passage in a sermon that someone watched online. The following week I received this email message: "Does that mean that Jesus said when you stand at the door and knock he says 'I don't LOVE you'? [to the writer's credit he/she remembered that "know" can be interpreted as "love."] Does not sound like my father. I will never not love my children. I do not believe he will ever stop loving me!"

I really appreciate that question because it means that some are listening and trying to process this with me, even though this listener misunderstood my meaning. So let's break this down and see if we should translate this Matthew 7 passage as "I don't love you" and whether that would be consistent with "God so loved the world that He gave..." John 3:16

Jesus is clear in this Matthew 7 passage that, just because you accept Jesus and call him "Lord, Lord," heaven is not guaranteed. In fact, some making that profession will hear from Jesus in the judgment: "I never knew you. Away from me, you evildoers." Does that mean that He is saying to them "I never loved you"?

Now at first glance this seems out of character for Jesus. Is this the same Jesus who told the parable of the prodigal son where God is depicted as the ever-loving father who waits and longs for his rebellious son to return? And when he finally comes home, the father runs to him, hugs him and throws a party. Is Jesus holding back on us? Should He also have told a second prodigal son story? One where the father closes and locks the door when the son comes home knocking? One where the father says, "I don't love you. You evil son: I disown you"?

Let's put the puzzle together and see what picture of God develops. First, are we all sons and daughters of God? Yes we are, whether as lost children or saved children.[36] Did Jesus die for everyone? Yes. Did He do it because He loves us? Yes. Thus, our first piece of the puzzle is to recognize that if Jesus said, "I never loved you" it would be an incorrect interpretation because Jesus died for all because He DOES love all of us. In fact, "God demonstrates His own love toward us, in that while we were still sinners, Christ died for us." Romans 5:8 (NKJV)

Then we must ask, "Does Jesus stop loving us when we sin?" Let's look at that question. Toward the end of His ministry Jesus as He was talking with the Pharisees, with tears in His voice, cried out: "Jerusalem, Jerusalem, you who kill the prophets and stone those sent to you, how often I have longed to gather your children together, as a hen gathers her chicks under her wings, and you were not willing. Look, your house is left to you desolate." Matthew 23:37-38

And even hanging from the cross He cried out to the Father: "Father, forgive them, for they do not know what they do." Luke 23:34

Does that sound like Jesus still loves these people and their leaders who are crucifying Him? YES! In fact, it sounds exactly like the heart of the prodigal son's father. He weeps because He misses that loving fellowship with His people. In Matthew 23 Jesus seems to be crying out for His rebellious Jewish people,

---

[36] In the context of the salvation story we are created as sons and daughters of God. But through the fall of Adam and Eve and our own rebellious spirit we "gave ourselves" to Satan as his children. But Jesus by dying on the cross "redeemed" or "bought us back" from Satan and when we accept His sacrifice we are "adopted" into God's family as born again sons and daughters. As Paul wrote: *"You are not your own; you were bought at a price. Therefore honor God with your bodies."* 1 Corinthians 6:20

"What more could I have done to draw you to my heart but you would not come."

Now let's read what precedes this painful lament of Jesus: read Matthew 23: 16-36. Here He cuts loose with intense frustration and pain and repeatedly calls the Pharisees "hypocrites" and even "snakes and vipers." He recites a litany of their continued sins and abuses—committed IN THE NAME OF GOD! This is what immediately precedes his tearful cry of "Jerusalem, Jerusalem" which is another way of saying, "My children, my children," or "My son, my son I have loved you every way I know how but you will not come back to my heart." So, I think we can safely say that God does NOT stop loving us even when we in His name repeatedly abuse Him and His people.

Another thing to note about the Matthew 7 passage is that I assume that the author of the email message replaced the word "know" with "love," as could be done. However, a word study of this word that here is translated as "know" shows us that in some texts it is also means to "recognize" as in "I know (recognize) what I saw." We need to consider the context to determine a word's proper translation. In this Matthew 7 passage the word "know" must be referring to something other than "love". But, if we were to interpret "know" as "recognize" it would read, "I do not *recognize* you—that is, you do not have the characteristics or attitude of a kingdom-bound disciple." This wording makes a lot more contextual sense, doesn't it? And it is in harmony with God's character of love.

So, is it possible that the man in Matthew 7 who professed to be a follower of God seeking entrance into heaven is one of these same Pharisees? This man not only seeks entrance but (as implied) demands entrance by reminding God of the many awesome acts of ministry that obviously prove him to be a righteous man. But Jesus responds, "I don't recognize you as one of my disciples. You do not have the characteristics or attitude of a kingdom-bound disciple. Go away because you are an impostor."

Does that begin to make sense? Does Jesus send him away because He doesn't love him? No. Jesus turns him away because the imposter was pretending to be righteous. In fact, the Pharisees repeatedly abused their power by stealing from widows, neglecting orphans and teaching in manner that the common person lost all hope of heaven being reachable for them. Jesus pronounced the woes upon them to demonstrate how deceived they were and how different was Their character versus God's.

He didn't pronounce the woes to indicate He had stopped loving them because afterwords He broke down and wept for them. THAT is what a loving father does. He weeps over His lost children.

A reasonably correct conclusion of the Matthew 7 passage is that this man, as a religious leader, is demanding entrance by parading his awesome deeds which, he believes, proves that he is a citizen of heaven. But, although he IS a son of God (as a child of Adam and his Hebrew genealogy) and although Jesus loves him dearly, his righteousness is only superficial, self-seeking AND he has used his religious power to actually destroy other innocent people. He shows no sorrow for his sinful treachery, while still demanding entrance into heaven's rewards.[37]

Would YOU let such a person into heaven where he could ply his self-centered, destructive trade... even IF he were your son? God's love for all of us means that he MUST NOT allow this son into heaven where he will continue destroying other sons and daughters who are honestly seeking to love and serve God.

The Message Bible restates this passage in a manner that validates this interpretation:

---

[37] Compare this with my discussion of John 8 in Chapter 5 where the Pharisee were claiming to be "sons of Abraham" but Jesus said he didn't recognize them as such because they didn't do the works of Abraham but were doing the works of the Devil.

Knowing the correct password—saying "Master, Master," for instance—isn't going to get you anywhere with me. What is required is serious obedience—doing what my Father wills. I can see it now—at the Final Judgment thousands strutting up to me and saying, "Master, we preached the Message, we bashed the demons, our God-sponsored projects had everyone talking." And do you know what I am going to say? "You missed the boat. All you did was use me to make yourselves important. You don't impress me one bit. You're out of here."

Let's make this more personal. Let's say that you have three children (two sons and a daughter) and your eldest son is Robert, who is single and still lives in your home. Then one day you here this news break: *"Robert Pimental, a fourth grade teacher in Wilmington, CA, has been accused by 20 children and one adult of sexual abuse, the Los Angeles Police Department reported. The Los Angeles County District Attorney's Office filed eight counts of continuous sexual abuse and seven counts of lewd acts upon a child against Pimental."*

As if that news isn't devastating enough, you learn that one of the children he has been continuously abusing is your second grade daughter—born to you late in life. When confronted with the facts, Robert shows no sign of regret nor repentance. In fact he says, "Oh, the whole thing is blown out of proportion. Actually, some of these girls I think liked it. I probably did them a favor. And besides, I've done a lot of good things for that school and those young girls. They ought to be thanking me!"

Imagine yourself saying, "Robert, you're always my son and my love is constant so I MUST let you live here at home. And since our house is so small you can stay in the bedroom with your sister." NO! That's insanity!! That's NOT the response of a loving father.

The Whatever Factor

More likely you would say: "Son, I cannot let you live in our home. I love you and would do anything to change your heart, but you've become someone I don't really know. I cannot trust you nor let allow you to continue hurting your sister."

Perhaps you're uncomfortable that I am using this illustration. But if we were to talk frankly, with 100% honesty, we could share many such incidents with all of their ugly details that would turn your stomach. God sees the ugliness and knows every detail of the physical and emotional pain and its long term damaging effects. And He says "I HATE sin! Those who embrace and excuse it with a WHATever attitude I will never allow into heaven!"

So let's review: All of us are God's children and He loves each one, even when we sin... even when our sin is really BAD. But He is building a universe where there is one theme and one pulse beat of love and He will not... He must not... allow anyone into heaven who embraces and excuses sin in his or her life, because that pattern of destruction would be continued in heaven.

Now, those who ARE saved are NOT without sinful tendencies BUT the defining difference is their attitude toward sin. They have come to HATE sin in their life. They do NOT make excuses for sin nor have a flippant WHATever attitude toward it. Instead, they passionately want God's character to be recreated in them, AND they are in that process when Jesus returns. Thus, heaven for them is simply a continuation of their transformation process WITHOUT the interference of Satan nor the interference of other humans who think sin is no big deal. You could say that Phase I of their heaven is already in process "right now". And the "yet to come" Phase II begins when they arrive in heaven where they will continue to mature in Jesus' love and character.

"Okay, Pastor, I can see why Jesus might love a child abuser while not allowing him into heaven if his attitude doesn't change, but I'm not that kind of person. My sins are like minor league in comparison. Sure, I might gossip occasionally, or hold a grudge (which I have reason for), or shade the truth a bit (but it doesn't hurt anyone), or sleep with my girlfriend (no big deal because we're seriously in love), and I do community service (admittedly as much for my reputation in the community as it is a service of love but at least I do it). I might occasionally drink too much, or watch just a little porn... but those are little sins, no big deal. Besides, I actually DO a lot of things for the church and community and do love kids and do get emotional when I see a child or animal suffer... so Jesus would never say that to me. Or would He?"

So, you're saying that God doesn't worry about little sins, just big ones? Listen, God says that ANY sin is big because sin begins in the heart, the mind, the attitude. When in our mind we choose a WHATever attitude toward anything in opposition to God, THAT is big because that attitude is evidence of a spiritual cancer. And God knows that spiritual cancer, harbored, grows into greater pain and destruction.

Wasn't Lucifer's sin pretty small—persistently criticizing the way God ran things in heaven? And how big a sin was Adam's eating of the forbidden fruit? I mean, neither Lucifer's nor Adam's sin was like killing anyone or sexually abusing little girls. But their sin WAS a big deal because as a spiritual cancer it grew in succeeding generations into horrific destructive results resulting in sexual abuse of little second grade girls, concentration camps, torture, demonic possession, mass murders and more. No wonder God HATES sin... . big sin... little sin... ANY sin, because spiritual cancer is never a small thing.

Let me tell you a story. A few years ago a pilot was practicing high-speed maneuvers at a low altitude at night in a jet fighter with no visual reference points. She pulled back on the stick for what she thought was a steep ascent—and flew straight into the ground. She was unaware that she had been flying upside down. That in pilot's language is called vertigo or spatial disorientation. Hard to believe if you've never flown, but very believable if you have. In fact, the Air Force investigated 633 military crashes in the 1980s and discovered that 13% were the result of spatial disorientation which resulted in 115 deaths. That's why instructors always say, "Trust your instruments no matter what you're feeling."

That's a parable of our current human existence, including many professed Christians. Spiritually and morally they have no idea whether they're flying upside down or right side up. So they go by feel. If they feel that a sin is no big deal, then they BELIEVE it's no big deal. They fail to trust their instruments... which, of course, is God's Word in the Bible.

In fact, many Christians are beginning to believe that the Bible is NOT their only rule of faith... that it's old fashioned and antiquated. Therefore, they need to simply judge according to their own self-conceived standards of conduct. And when they see a majority of others around them thinking and acting the same (including Christians), then they KNOW they're justified. That's a definition of a Christian flying upside down. And when they make a move that they feel is right in their own eyes, they fly themselves into the ground.

The Bible speaks of this spiritual disorientation: "There is a way that appears to be right (in their own eyes), but in the end it leads to death." Proverbs 14:12. In another passage, "There is a generation that are pure in their own eyes, and yet is not washed from their filthiness. Proverbs 30:12 (ASV)

I think this could be speaking of our generation. So many Christians are flying upside down and telling themselves and each other that they're just fine and that their little infractions are no big deal and God's grace will overlook the minor stuff. That's a Christian that God cannot trust to bring into heaven. Thus he says, *"To KNOW me* (meaning to take time with me where you come to love me AND trust my Word as your only safe guide WHICH leads to my recreating my character in you WHICH results in your hating ANY sin against Me) . . "To know me IS eternal life." John 17:3

How Far Is Heaven? How Far Is God?

He IS always with us, around us and trying to love and guide us. But He wants to be more than just with and around us. He wants to be IN us through His Holy Spirit. Not just part of us part of the time, but dwelling fully in every part of our life. He wants us to be able to sing "Heaven came down and glory FILLED my soul." Meaning, Jesus is living IN my heart and I have a growing passion that He extend his living quarters and influence in my heart to include EVERY room of my life.

In fact, I want Paul's motto to be mine: "WhatEVER I eat or whatEVER I drink or whatEVER I do, I want to do for the glory of God." Which means that I hate ANY sin in my life and don't want to nurture anything that resists the dwelling of God in my life. That is the attitude of the person who is flying right side up, en route to heaven.

THAT's the attitude I want to define my life and to define yours as well. But that won't happen without honest and persistent evaluation of what we treasure most and how *that* treasure dictates the priorities of our life.

Imagination Station #12

How about snowboarding in heaven?

Let's have some fun. Pretend that you and your friends have just completed a century of learning from Jesus about fractals. Then someone in your group says, "You know, Lord, one thing I kind of miss is snow. The few times I was able to go skiing and snowboarding, it was a blast. I've looked around, but Mount Zion doesn't have snow and the climate is so... well, so moderate here. I kind of miss my snow."

Jesus' whole countenance reverberates with light and energy as He asks, "So how many of you would like to go skiing? Well, follow me." You don't need rocket packs with the heavenly ability to blast off, do several barrel rolls and loops, plunge into the sea and chase some dolphins, before surging out of the water and off across the vast universe.

After shooting through a million light years of space at warp speed, Jesus stops in the midst of a vast cosmic vacuum and says, "This looks like a good place for a snow galaxy." With a word and sweep of His hand, Jesus creates a whole galaxy of snow planets.

"So, let's check out my handiwork," He says, blasting through the atmosphere of the first planet and easing down onto the tallest, most awesome mountain ever envisioned. "Are you ready?" And off He goes. No need for a snowboard or skis because all you need is imagine your desired shape and size and change it for every run. And if you're a sissy about the cold, don't worry. The snow is any temperature you like, climate controlled according to each person's comfort level. And, remember: there's no more pain, so don't worry about falling. In fact, falls are often the most fun.

After a few awesome runs He says, "Well, that's just a start. I got some creative ideas on this run." And, again, you're off. But this time everything is different. Remember: snow is made of ice crystals... CRYSTALS!

Crystals are miniature prisms that refract the light into a rainbow of colors. As you make those sweeping turns and shoot a wall of snow hundreds of feet into the air, they refract the light into millions of dancing rainbows.

Oh, just before this run, Jesus sweeps His hand and creates six more suns, each emitting a different light spectrum. So now the dancing rainbows of snow crystals have colors, shapes, and reverberating characteristics NEVER before imagined. To be continued...

Chapter 13:

The Whatever Factor Reaches into Your Wallet

"Do not lay up for yourselves treasures on earth, where moth and rust destroy and where thieves break in and steal; but lay up for yourselves treasures in heaven, where neither moth nor rust destroys and where thieves do not break in and steal. For where your treasure is, there your heart will be also."[38] Jesus

Everyone has treasures.[39] That is an essential part of what it is to be human.

Nothing degrades people more than to scorn, destroy, or deprive us of our treasures. Treasures are directly connected to our dignity and sense of security. In fact, a special part of friendship and/or marriage intimacy is to discover and honor what the other really treasures.

---

[38] Matthew 6:19-21 (NKJV).

[39] I thankfully give credit to Dr. Dallas Willard, the author of *The Divine Conspiracy* for enriching some of my thoughts in this chapter.

The Whatever Factor Reaches into Your Wallet

Before I was of school age one of my personal treasurers was a blanket, i.e, my "bwanky". I found it in a box of stuff left in a summer cabin in a logging camp where my dad worked for a few months. "Summer cabin" is probably too complimentary. It was not a vacation villa. It was constructed of boards with no paint, no insulation, no sheet rock, just bare wood walls with cracks you could see through. The windows were holes in the wood with plastic draped over them. No plumbing (an outhouse and creek), no electricity (a kerosene lantern), no heating (just more blankets)—and northern California nights in the mountains do get cold.

But it became our home. The first day we walked in, amidst the dust, there was a box in the corner which contained a small dirty blanket—like a baby blanket with a little padding and a soft rope-like border on the edges. I latched onto that and for years it was my treasure. I couldn't sleep unless my bwanky was in bed with me where I could fuzz the ropy edge with my finger. My mom reminds me that she cut it into quarters so it would last longer. I've been told, maybe it's true, that even into my early teens, I sneaked my bwanky into bed without others seeing or laughing.

It WAS my childhood treasure. What was yours? A doll, a stuffed animal, a pet? What is your treasure now? It's normal to have one and to keep it rather secret. Or, maybe you want your treasures to be obvious to everyone: jewelry, house, adult toys, etc. We reveal our treasures by what we protect and secure. They may be worthless to others but often not—such as money, wealth, good looks, and material goods.

The first thing Jesus says about our treasures upon the earth is that by nature they cannot be held intact. Moth destroys, time ages, constant use wears away, cars fall apart, homes destroyed. That's why investing in precious metals, gold, and silver is so popular today. Many believe that the dollar, because of the government's out of control spending and printing of billions of dollars with no gold to secure it, will soon crash and be worth

50% or maybe even 20% of its current value. So many buy gold. And what will you do with that?

Of course, gold won't lose its investment value like paper money, but will you buy bread or gas with it? It's worthless when sitting in your safe. It's like a stuffed animal or bwanky: it makes one feel secure. It's only worth what someone is willing to pay or trade for it. AND it can be stolen, maybe at gunpoint.

So we have our little securities, but what is your primary security? Or do you treasure God and living with Him in heaven more than anything else? Can your primary security be taken by moths or the economy or thieves? Is it even your children or your spouse? They too can be taken away, can they not?

The only things of value that cannot be taken are your character and your faith. You can lose those only by your choice. So Jesus challenges us to not just look at the surface, but look beyond. Look deeper. Regarding money and earthly securities, recognize that they can disappear. So go deeper. Go to the heart. Character and faith reside in your heart and it's in your heart that you love God, love yourself and others. Invest in those heart issues.

That's the primary reason God asks us to give 10% of our income as a tithe offering. It's why He asks us to be generous with the rest of our money, our time, and our energies. Because our heart is naturally selfish, it hoards attention, money and things and the acceptance and praise of others. It also hoards securities. But when we give quietly and without a craving for reward, that unselfish act serves as an antibiotic to our selfish hearts.

The amount of our gift is not most important. It's what we have left after we give the gift that determines our sacrifice. If I have 5 million dollars and give $100,000 I still have 4.9 million and I could probably live comfortably on that... for a while. But if I have 10 pennies and give 2 away, then the gift is great. That's why Jesus said of the widow who gave her 2 mites, "Her gift was far greater than those who gave from their wealth."

(Mark 12:43) Maybe the person with 5 million needs to give 4 million away before it becomes an unselfish gift. Make sense? How much do you need to give away before money and investments are no longer your primary security? Bottom line: We give until our primary treasure is no longer in the bank or in our wardrobe or jewelry box or garage. Rather, we keep giving away until our heart tells us that our treasure—our security—is now in the heart and care of God, not in something we have hoarded.

Organizing Our Lives around Our Treasures

Whatever our treasure, around that we organize our lives. If it's around investments, then our life is organized around that. Or cars, or music, or our good looks, body tone, make-up then we organize around those things. If it's our children, we go berzerk and lose our Christianity if anyone criticizes or belittles them. Yes, we work hard for money, plan well for investments, try to look our best, and love our children, but around what or who do we organize our life? That tells us where our primary treasure is. If it's around anything or anyone except God, then we WILL lose it sooner or later... perhaps for eternity.

For our personal lives, the Apostle Paul explains Jesus' statement about "where your treasure is, there your heart will be also":

> Whatever were gains to me I now consider loss for the sake of Christ. What is more, I consider everything a loss because of the surpassing worth of knowing Christ Jesus my Lord, for whose sake I have lost all things. I consider them garbage, that I may gain Christ and be found in him, not having a righteousness of my own that comes from the law, but that which is through faith in Christ—the righteousness

that comes from God on the basis of faith. I want to know Christ—yes, to know the power of his resurrection and participation in his sufferings, becoming like him in his death, and so, somehow, attaining to the resurrection from the dead.

Not that I have already obtained all this, or have already arrived at my goal, but I press on to take hold of that for which Christ Jesus took hold of me. Brothers and sisters, I do not consider myself yet to have taken hold of it. But one thing I do: Forgetting what is behind and straining toward what is ahead, I press on toward the goal to win the prize for which God has called me heavenward in Christ Jesus. All of us, then, who are mature should take such a view of things. Philippians 3:7-15

I love what he is saying. Of all people, Paul—that great apostle—puts into two paragraphs the whatEVER factor with clarity. First, he knows he is not perfect. Second, he still KNOWS he is heaven bound. Third, why does he know? Because he's settled in his own heart that his primary investment is loving God and becoming like Him. It's nothing here on earth. Rather, it is to know, serve and become like Jesus. In comparison everything else is valued as garbage.

In that context Paul's whatEVER statement makes a lot more sense: "Therefore, whether you eat or drink, or whatEVER you do, do all to the glory of God." 1 Corinthians 10:31 (NKJV)

Coming back to Jesus' lessons about our treasures, we read in Matthew 6:24 (MSG): "You can't worship two gods at once. Loving one god, you'll end up hating the other. Adoration of one feeds contempt for the other. You can't worship both God and money."

It's another way of stating the first commandment: "You shall have no other gods before me." That's not an arbitrary dictatorial command. It's a protective statement. "Please, let me be your primary security, the only one who really gives you value, and the only one who secures your future. Any other treasure that holds your heart will someday escape your grasp and could cost you eternity."

Then Jesus promises that worry over our food and clothes should not consume us:

> If you decide for God, living a life of God-worship, it follows that you don't fuss about what's on the table at mealtimes or whether the clothes in your closet are in fashion. There is far more to your life than the food you put in your stomach, more to your outer appearance than the clothes you hang on your body. Look at the birds, free and unfettered, not tied down to a job description, careless in the care of God. And you count far more to him than birds. Has anyone by fussing in front of the mirror ever gotten taller by so much as an inch? All this time and money wasted on fashion—do you think it makes that much difference? Instead of looking at the fashions, walk out into the fields and look at the wildflowers. They never primp or shop, but have you ever seen color and design quite like it? The ten best-dressed men and women in the country look shabby alongside them.
>
> If God gives such attention to the appearance of wildflowers—most of which are never even seen—don't you think he'll attend to you, take

pride in you, do his best for you? What I'm trying to do here is to get you to relax, to not be so preoccupied with getting, so you can respond to God's giving. People who don't know God and the way he works fuss over these things, but you know both God and how he works... Give your entire attention to what God is doing right now, and don't get worked up about what may or may not happen tomorrow. God will help you deal with whatever hard things come up when the time comes. Matthew 6:25-34 (MSG)

The Apostle Paul echoes this in Philippians 4:19 (MEV): "My God shall supply every need you have." Some think this means that if we have the right formula for prayer, or the right kind of faith, or make the right pilgrimage or give an adequate seed offering that we shall never be cold, go hungry, be sick or without shelter. If that's your interpretation, then you have failed to look deeper, failed to look beyond the obvious.

Jesus makes it clear in the Gospels that we are not exempt from the normal problems of life. We are not exempt from sickness, hunger, imprisonment, harm, or violent death, although there are occasions where God intervenes with a miracle. It doesn't mean that if we pray the right formula or spin the correct prayer wheel or fast long enough, we will be able to fully enjoy what all Americans want, i.e., life, liberty and the pursuit of happiness... unencumbered and with a minimum of sacrifice and effort.

Jesus is not suggesting that this side of heaven we will have all of these in their fullest. Indeed, there will be times when we have no friends, our marriage fails, our children turn away, our money dissipates and our bwanky wears out. Rather, Jesus is teaching that in such cases we will be unshaken.

In essence Jesus promises: "Life is hard in this world, and also will be hard for my followers. But cheer up! I have overcome the world. You will never lose more than I lost, but I was unshaken because my security, my heart, my treasure was in my Father. My security could not be taken away. And now, I live where my treasure and security were invested. I live in my Father's presence.

You too, have the same promise. If your treasure and heart is in heaven, in Me and my Father's love and promises for you, then you can relax your death grip on everything here on earth and hold onto me. You too can organize your life around me and not around your treasurers. And you too will someday be rewarded a hundred times over by living in My presence and enjoying awesome things together that defy your imagination... and your cup will run over with joy as you dwell in My Father's house forever."

Sometimes the lens of our heart needs to be refocused on what is REALLY important. We're like the blind man whose eyes Jesus had to touch a second time so he could see clearly:

> He took the blind man by the hand and led him outside the village. When he had spit on the man's eyes and put his hands on him, Jesus asked, "Do you see anything?"
>
> He looked up and said, "I see people; they look like trees walking around."
>
> Once more Jesus put his hands on the man's eyes. Then his eyes were opened, his sight was restored, and he saw everything clearly. Mark 8:23-25

The whatEVER attitude is key to refocusing your heart. If your passion is that Jesus will touch your "eyes" yet again so you can clearly see what He wants you to become, then your whatEVER attitude will fully embrace the power of the Holy

Spirit to accomplish this in your heart and mind resulting in you becoming the answer to Jesus' Gethsemane prayer. And what is that? It's a beautiful story that encompasses the whole Bible. It's a love story waiting for you in the next chapter.

Imagination Station #13

For those who have never skied in deep powder (like in the Rocky Mountains), it's like being in another world. You don't ski ON ungroomed powder but IN the snow, almost with a sense of slow motion. The snow is so dry and light it feels less like wet snow pellets and more like powdered sugar. It blows up, past your face and goggles. You sink in, then emerge up and over... then down again.

But ice crystals are... CRYSTALS. Ever snapped your fingernail against a stemmed glass to see if it's really crystal? Ding! Music! When snowboarding on earth that big swath of splayed snow crystals just sounded like a big "whooosh." But now that chaotic "whoosh" fractal sound becomes musical tones that cover ten times the sound spectrum then we've ever heard.

SO, down the hill you go with Jesus and your friends. You each sweep huge arches across the limitless deep snow. And you discover that you can create your own light and music show by manipulating the crystals with each slalom cut. In fact, all of you start working together to orchestrate a vast symphony of sound and lights. A whole new, ethereal, mystical, enchanting experience that is giving praise to Jesus.

You are so engrossed in your light and music show that Jesus has to shout it twice: "Open your mouth!" I mean, you're so deep in the powder that it's like you're floating through a cloud. The powdered sugar-like flakes burst up and over you. Then you open your mouth. **Chocolate... ice cream!** *AWESOME! A light and sound show skiing through fluffy light deep rich chocolate ice cream. What an awesome lunch! (And low fat!)*

When you finally reach the bottom, Jesus turns with a big smile and asks, "How about THAT! Anyone for chocolate mint?

That slope over there. Mango, over there. Espresso, back there. And that slope is create-your-own-flavor. Oh, if you want something really extreme, over there is Rocky Road, where you can jump off cliffs 10,000 high and soar for minutes before landing in the ice cream powder. Okay, so which one is it?"

"*Eye hath not seen, nor ear heard, neither have entered into the heart of man, the things which God hath prepared for them that love him.*"

Section V:
Whatever Is Forever

Chapter 14:

Heaven Is For People Whom Jesus Would Enjoy Forever

"Heaven is for people who are both loyal and loving... people Jesus would enjoy living with forever." The author

Garrison Keillor and his stories of Lake Woebegone have nothing over the small church where I grew up. I have many fond memories, some of which feature some pretty interesting folks.

I think of Dr. Diefenbaker, a dentist, who none of the kids really liked (after all, he WAS a dentist) except for one quirk. He sat on the center isle in church about three rows back and precisely at 12 o'clock he'd pull out his big gold pocket watch on a chain and begin swinging it back and forth in the aisle. We kids would think, "Yes! It's time for the preacher to stop so we can go free!"

Then there was Harold Hull. Seems there was nothing that Harold didn't think he could do. There was this tall pine tree; it was in the way, so Harold said, "I've got a chainsaw. I can cut it down." So he starts notching and cutting. My dad says, "Harold, I think it's going to fall against that other tree."

"Oh, no. I know what I'm doing."

Sure enough, it fell right on that adjoining pine tree and stuck at about a 45 degree angle. Well, Harold can do anything. So he clamped on his climbing spikes and up the uncut tree he went. Hanging on for dear life, he used his foot to push and push, but the other tree wouldn't dislodge. So Harold crawled over onto the leaning tree and pushed some more. Sure enough! It cut loose and down it came with Harold riding it like a bucking bronco. There was this huge crash and cloud of dust. Harold's steel helmet came fluttering down into the cloud. My dad thought he was dead, but soon there was this groan. Harold always survived.

As a child two things I remember that the church emphasized were, first, you must become perfect. Matthew 5:48: "Be perfect, therefore, as your heavenly Father is perfect." It was a very conservative, behavior-oriented approach to Christianity. You needed to get your life together, discipline yourself, and become perfect like God.

The second emphasis was to make converts. Matthew 28:19-20: "Therefore go and make disciples of all nations, teaching them to obey everything I have commanded you." You'd better start acting like a Christian or you won't be saved AND you'd better tell folks that they need to straighten up their lives as well—or they will be lost and it will be *your* fault!

And in so many ways I heard that whatever we were doing just wasn't enough: "Beloved, you know that you should be more committed, you should give more money, you should be more faithful in working for the church, you should stop drinking, smoking, cussing, playing cards, dancing, wearing makeup and jewelry, spending money on fancy clothes, etc, etc. And you should be convincing more people to get serious and change their life."

The Most-Religious-Person Award Goes to...

I felt far from being as spiritual as all that seemed. So I looked around to see who in the church might fit the bill. Who seemed really, really religious. Well, guess who? It was Mrs. Smith (not her real name). She was the one who sat in the front row of the choir and nodded her head when the preacher said all of this stuff and would "Amen. AMEN!" She carried her Bible everywhere and talked about long periods of study and prayer. She never entered into frivolous play or joking. She carried her bearing like a woman on her way to martyrdom at the stake, head bowed in an attitude of prayer.

Surely, she was the most perfectly religious person in the church. Trouble was, in my opinion she was one of the meanest persons in church. I always felt an air of being judged around her. If I were to have a birthday party, she would have been the last person on my invitation list. She could rain on anyone's parade. Plus, her son was in my class at school, and I heard of some pretty severe beatings at her hands. Have you ever noticed how sometimes the most pious, religious person can be the least pleasant to be around? Jesus found that to be true of Pharisees, so he hung out with "sinners, prostitutes and tax collectors."

Fortunately, as the years passed the Lord led me to embrace a more attractive Gospel, including a Scriptural passage that has completely changed my view of what the Bible is all about, what God wants me to be and what he wishes for me to emphasize in my ministry. So before I share that transforming text, let me give you a biblical backdrop.

I've come to learn that basically the Bible is all about one story. Some say it's a story of the great controversy between Jesus and Satan, good and evil, light and darkness. That is true. But I believe the story is much more intimate than that of a cosmic battle. The biblical story is of a loving God on a relentless search for a loving and faithful, spiritual wife... defined as a group of loving and loyal people whom He will enjoy living with forever.

God's Search for a Loving, Loyal Wife

The metaphor of God searching for a loving wife starts in the Old Testament. We pick up this story in Ezekiel 16:1. According to the book, the prophet Ezekiel was exiled in Babylon and experienced a series of seven visions during the 22 years from 593 to 571 BC, a period which spans the final destruction of Jerusalem in 586 BC.

Ezekiel writes this (The words in parentheses are mine):

> The word of the LORD came to me: "Son of man, confront Jerusalem with her detestable practices and say, 'This is what the Sovereign LORD says to Jerusalem: Your ancestry and birth were in the land of the Canaanites; your father was an Amorite and your mother a Hittite. On the day you were born your cord was not cut, nor were you washed with water to make you clean, nor were you rubbed with salt or wrapped in cloths. No one looked on you with pity or had compassion enough to do any of these things for you. Rather, you were thrown out into the open field, for on the day you were born you were despised. (In other words, Israel was an unwanted "dumpster baby" thrown into a field to die.)
>
> "Then I passed by and saw you kicking about in your blood, and as you lay there in your blood I said to you, 'Live!' I made you grow like a plant of the field. You grew and developed and entered puberty. Your breasts had formed and your hair had grown, yet you were stark naked.

"Later I passed by, and when I looked at you and saw that you were old enough for love, I spread the corner of my garment over you and covered your nakedness. I gave you my solemn oath and entered into a covenant with you, declares the Sovereign LORD, and you became mine. (This means she was old enough to enter into a marriage covenant; thus she became God's spiritual wife.)

"I bathed you with water and washed the blood from you and put ointments on you. I clothed you with an embroidered dress and put sandals of fine leather on you. I dressed you in fine linen and covered you with costly garments. I adorned you with jewelry: I put bracelets on your arms and a necklace around your neck, and I put a ring on your nose, earrings on your ears and a beautiful crown on your head.

"So you were adorned with gold and silver; your clothes were of fine linen and costly fabric and embroidered cloth. Your food was honey, olive oil and the finest flour. You became very beautiful and rose to be a queen. And your fame spread among the nations on account of your beauty, because the splendor I had given you made your beauty perfect, declares the Sovereign LORD. (His wife, now bejeweled, fed, clothed, was adored and envied as if she were a queen: all because of the gifts God had given to her.)

"But you trusted in your beauty and used your fame to become a prostitute. You lavished your favors on anyone who passed by and your beauty became his. You took some of your garments to make gaudy high places, where you carried on your prostitution. You went to him, and he possessed your beauty. You also took the fine jewelry I gave you, the jewelry made of my gold and silver, and you made for yourself male idols and engaged in prostitution with them. And you took your embroidered clothes to put on them, and you offered my oil and incense before them. Also the food I provided for you—the flour, olive oil and honey I gave you to eat—you offered as fragrant incense before them. That is what happened, declares the Sovereign Lord.

"And you took your sons and daughters whom you bore to me and sacrificed them as food to the idols. Was your prostitution not enough? You slaughtered my children and sacrificed them to the idols. In all your detestable practices and your prostitution you did not remember the days of your youth, when you were naked and bare, kicking about in your blood.

"'Woe! Woe to you,' declares the Sovereign LORD. In addition to all your other wickedness, you built a mound for yourself and made a lofty shrine in every public square. At every street corner you built your lofty shrines and degraded your beauty, spreading your legs with increasing promiscuity to anyone who passed by. You engaged in prostitution with the Egyptians, your neighbors with large genitals, and aroused my anger with your increasing promiscuity. So I stretched out my hand against you and reduced your territory; I gave you over to the greed of your enemies, the daughters of the Philistines, who were shocked by your lewd conduct. You engaged in prostitution with the Assyrians too, because you were insatiable; and even after that, you still were not satisfied. Then you increased your promiscuity to include Babylonia, a land of merchants, but even with this you were not satisfied.

"I am filled with fury against you, declares the Sovereign LORD, when you do all these things, acting like a brazen prostitute! When you built your mounds at every street corner and made your lofty shrines in every public square, you were unlike a prostitute, because you scorned payment.

"You adulterous wife! You prefer strangers to your own husband! All prostitutes receive gifts, but you give gifts to all your lovers, bribing them to come to you from everywhere for your illicit favors. So in your prostitution you are the opposite of others; no one runs after you for your favors. You are the very opposite, for you give payment and none is given to you.

"Therefore, you prostitute, hear the word of the LORD! This is what the Sovereign LORD says: 'Because you poured out your lust and exposed your nakedness in your promiscuity with your lovers, and because of all your detestable idols, and because you gave them your children's blood, therefore I am going to gather all your lovers, with whom you found pleasure, those you loved as well as those you hated. I will gather them against you from all around and will strip you in front of them, and they will see all your nakedness. I will sentence you to the punishment of women who commit adultery and who shed blood; I will bring on you the blood vengeance of my wrath and jealous anger. Then I will deliver you into the hands of your lovers, and they will tear down your mounds and destroy your lofty shrines. They will strip you of your clothes and take your fine jewelry and leave you naked and bare.'"

Isaiah 3 is a parallel passage to this text where God speaks of stripping his wife of her jewels, her fine clothes, her health, and her gourmet food. Why is God upset? Because the gifts He has given her as an expression of His love have been used in affairs with other lovers. That is, she uses these gifts in her worship of idols, which is spiritual adultery. And if that isn't enough, she actually offers their children as sacrifices to these adulterous idols.

Many of the Old Testament prophets sing a similar song of warning and woe. In fact, to help Hosea understand the gut-wrenching pain of God in dealing with His adulterous Israelite wife, He told Hosea to marry a prostitute and learn firsthand the pain God was experiencing: "Go, marry a promiscuous woman and have children with her, for like an adulterous wife this land is guilty of unfaithfulness to the Lord." Hosea 1:2

In this Ezekiel passage, Israel's spiritual adultery has been going on/off for around eight hundred years. God is so patient with his wife. Time and again she is seduced by idol worship and repeatedly God calls call her back home, forgive and love her again. Of course, each time she returns she says, "I'm so sorry. I'll never I'll never worship idols again." But she does.

God Sends His Adulterous "Wife" Away

Finally, God essentially says, "Okay, if you're so enamored by other gods, I'm going to let you go live with the mother of all idolatrous nations, the nation of Babylon. Live with your lover and see what it's really like." Babylon in the Bible is the symbol of idolatry and adulterous false worship, even in the New Testament book of Revelation. So in approximately 600 BC King Nebuchadnezzar from Babylon conquered Jerusalem and hauled them off to live as captives.

Remember that Jerusalem was the city where God was to dwell in love and peace with his "wife." And the temple symbolized their home. So when Nebuchadnezzar destroyed both their city and their temple, it was symbolic of the destructive effects of adultery.

Soon the Israelites were sitting on the banks of the River Euphrates singing songs of lament (as recorded in the Book of Lamentations) where they longed to go home to Jerusalem and to their God. Finally, under the leadership of Ezra, Nehemiah and Zachariah God brought His battered and bruised wife home and they rebuilt the temple. She had been a very unfaithful idolatrous wife, so God said, "I'll bring you home if you promise never to go whoring after other gods again." And she agreed AND kept that promise. Many of the Old Testament prophecies about Israel's return and promised prosperity were fulfilled at this time, but because of Israel's lack of heart relationship with Yahweh, not all the glowing prophetic promises could be fulfilled.

I'm not aware of any record of Israel falling into idolatry after her return from Babylonian captivity. She was going to be a "faithful" wife, do her duty, and keep the rules. In fact, she elevated the teaching of Torah by creating hundreds of man-made rules along with lists of do's and don'ts that, if observed, would keep her from slipping back into idolatry. Or so she thought.

But a marriage based on a list of rules without a loving relationship is not one to be enjoyed. You might say God's wife had become loyal, but, in the process, had become frigid. For her, marriage was a duty. Religion was very structured and controlling. She now was "loyal" but her heart was not into the "loving" part. Remember, God is searching for a wife that is both loyal and loving.

Jesus Luring His Wife Back

So when Jesus came and walked the dusty pathways of Palestine and taught in the temple and synagogues, He was trying to convince His frigid wife to loosen up and enjoy a love relationship with Him.

You never hear Jesus saying that His wife should be more loyal by keeping the rules better. Jesus wanted not just a loyal wife, but also a loving one. One who loved intimacy and laughed and played. Jesus said, "You have your heads in your Bibles constantly because you think you'll find eternal life there. But you miss the forest for the trees. These Scriptures are all about me! And here I am, standing right before you, and you aren't willing to receive from me the life you say you want." John 5:39 (MSG) He tried to woo her heart for over three years, but at the end of His ministry Jesus wept, realizing that all of His efforts had not successfully healed their marriage.

During His final week He cleansed the temple by saying, "My house will be a house of prayer." Matthew 21:13 But a few days later He tells the Jewish leaders: "Have you never read in the Scriptures: 'The stone the builders rejected has become the cornerstone; the Lord has done this, and it is marvelous in our eyes'? Therefore I tell you that the kingdom of God will be taken away from you and given to a people who will produce its fruit. (Meaning the New Testament church made up of believing Jews and Gentiles). Anyone who falls on this stone will be broken to pieces, but anyone on whom it falls will be crushed." Matthew 21:42-44

Then shortly thereafter, just hours before His crucifixion, in the temple compound where these conversations often transpired, Jesus weeps, "Oh, Jerusalem, Jerusalem (my love, my love), you who kill the prophets and stone those sent to you, how often I have longed to gather your children together, as a hen gathers her chicks under her wings, and you were not willing. Look, your house is left to you desolate..." Matthew 23:37-38

Interesting transition of words. A short time earlier He still called the temple "My house," but now He changes it to "your house." That is a statement of divorce. With tears in His voice, He is saying, "I have done everything possible to draw you to my heart, but you would not come. So, you get the house; I'm leaving. It was OUR house at one time but it's over. I must find a true wife who understands heartfelt love and not just obedience. There's nothing more I can do." One might say that Israel later signed the divorce by crucifying her Husband.[40]

Jesus Searches for a New Wife

But God is on a relentless search for a wife that is both loving and loyal. So He keeps searching. And in the New Testament His new bride is the church, composed of both believing Jews and Gentiles. The Apostle Paul recognized this new church as God's new bride in 2 Corinthians 11:2: "I am jealous for you with a godly jealousy. I promised you to one husband, to Christ, so that I might present you as a pure virgin to him."

This new bride would not be defined by genealogy or race or status. but by her faithfulness and, especially, by her love. Paul writes to the Gentile Galatians: "So in Christ Jesus you

---

[40] God's dramatic act of ripping the temple curtain from top to bottom (Matthew 17:51) was a visual demonstration that He no longer considered the temple His dwelling place.

are all children of God through faith, for all of you who were baptized into Christ have clothed yourselves with Christ. There is neither Jew nor Gentile, neither slave nor free, neither male nor female, for you are all one in Christ Jesus. If you belong to Christ, then you are Abraham's seed, and heirs according to the promise." Galatians 3:26-29

And again in Romans 2:28-29 (NKJV): "For he is not a Jew who is one outwardly, nor is circumcision that which is outward in the flesh; but he is a Jew who is one inwardly; and circumcision is that of the heart, in the Spirit, not in the letter; whose praise is not from men but from God."

He was seeking a wife (a church) that was both faithful AND loving. The Apostle Paul makes it clear that there were faithful and loving Jews who would form the nucleus of this new church to which believing Gentiles would be added. The church was NOT a Gentile church, but a combination—with Jews being converted FIRST, then the Gentiles. "For I am not ashamed of this Good News about Christ. It is the power of God at work, saving everyone who believes—the Jew **first** and also the Gentile." Romans 1:16 (NLT)

Jesus' Dying Prayer for His New Wife

BUT what might that church (new wife) and its people look like, other than a mixture of Jews and Gentiles?

All of what we have studied so far brings me to the passage that has transformed my ministry: John 17:17-23 The context of this prayer of Jesus is in the Garden of Gethsemane the night before His crucifixion. You know, when someone knows they are dying, their final words and final requests are pretty important. They are worth some special attention. Here is Jesus' dying request: actually, three requests, which are sequential.

His first request: Vs. 15-17: "My prayer is not that you take them out of the world but that you protect them from the evil one. They are not of the world, even as I am not of it. Sanctify them by the truth; your word is truth." We will see in a few verses that He is not only praying for His remaining disciples but "for those who will believe in me through their message," which includes all of His believers down to our day.

What does it mean to be sanctified? In my incorrect childhood understanding of sanctification, I needed to live a perfect life of do's and don'ts: "Be perfect, therefore, as your heavenly Father is perfect." Matthew 5:48

But, I thought further, what does this word "sanctify" REALLY mean. So I looked at other passages where this word was used. Here are some examples:

The first time is in Genesis 2:3 (KJV): "Then God blessed the seventh day and sanctified it, because in it He rested from all His work which God had created and made." Hmmm, here I see that time was sanctified.

Then in Exodus 13:2 (KJV) I found that God said the first born of Israel must be sanctified unto the Lord: "Sanctify unto me all the firstborn, whatsoever openeth the womb among the children of Israel, both of man and of beast: it is mine." Hmmm, even people and beasts were sanctified by an act of dedication.

Then I found that Moses sanctified the people of Israel: "And Moses went down from the mount unto the people, and sanctified the people; and they washed their clothes." Exodus 19:14 (KJV)

Then in Leviticus 8:10 (KJV) I read: "And Moses took the anointing oil, and anointed the tabernacle and all that was therein, and sanctified them." So "things" like the tabernacle and its utensils and furnishings were sanctified. What did that mean? More biblical examples could be quoted with this word "sanctify."

So I checked *Cruden's Concordance* for a definition of *sanctify*: *"To separate and appoint anything to a holy and religious use."*

Well, that seemed clear. So when the Sabbath time, the first born, the people of Israel, or the items in the tabernacle were "sanctified," it meant that they were "separated from the common and appointed for a holy use."

Therefore, in Jesus' Gethsemane prayer, He pleads with His Father that we who believe would recognize that we have been "sanctified," i.e., separated out from the world for a holy use. For what kind of holy use?

Well, why was the tabernacle sanctified? Exodus 29:43 (KJV): "The tabernacle shall be sanctified *for my glory.*"

So the tabernacle was sanctified, separated out, for the glory of God, i.e., for His presence. His sanctifying presence was also very visible, seen first as a pillar of fire at night and a cloud by day hovering over the tabernacle and people. He wanted to dwell in HIS tabernacle. That's why it was sanctified. It was set apart so God could dwell therein in a special manner to accomplish a holy purpose.

Is that what it means for us to sanctified? Are we declared to be sanctified—set apart—for God's special presence so we can accomplish a holy purpose? Paul believes so, because he talks about us being God's temple wherein He wishes to dwell: "Don't you know that you yourselves are God's temple and that God's Spirit dwells in your midst?" 1 Corinthians 3:16

1 Corinthians 6:19-20: "Do you not know that your bodies are temples of the Holy Spirit, who is in you, whom you have received from God? You are not your own; you were bought at a price."

Being Sanctified Means Being "Set Apart"

Then what? For what purpose? What difference does that make in your life? Will it be noticeable? Will His presence in your life be visible, like the pillar of fire or cloud? Well, yes, it will be visible—not with a cloud hovering above you but by the transformation that He accomplishes in your heart.

Paul refers to God's indwelling presence as the Holy Spirit residing in our hearts. And His presence is noticeable because

He ALWAYS produces beautiful and obvious fruit: "The fruit of the Spirit is love, joy, peace, patience, kindness, goodness, faithfulness, gentleness and self-control." Galatians 5:22-23 Of course, this is a definition of the character of Jesus.

In other words, the Holy Spirit dwelling in our heart will always and naturally transform our characters to be like that of Jesus. Like the Apostle John said, "He who says he abides in Him ought himself also to walk just as He walked." 1 John 2:6 (NKJV)

Okay, so to be sanctified means that we are set apart as God's temple to be filled with His Holy Spirit. And the evidence of that will be an obvious and growing manifestation of love, joy, peace, patience, kindness, goodness, faithfulness, gentleness, and self-control. That sure feels a lot different than trying hard to behave as a perfect Christian.

That was the first request of Jesus in His dying Gethsemane prayer. Notice what follows: "My prayer is not for them alone. I pray also for those who will believe in me through their message (that means every believer), that all of them may be one, Father, just as you are in me and I am in you." John 17:20-21

Five times in this chapter Jesus prays for oneness among His followers. That repetition demands our attention. Could it be that He emphasized it because it is so ignored, yet so very important?

Notice that most of the Fruit of the Holy Spirit are relational. Love is something that is expressed within community. A peaceable spirit is seen in the midst of conflict between people. Gentleness, goodness and kindness are how we treat someone else. So when you have individuals who are growing in these attributes, and they come together in a faith community, you will see a community defined by how they love each other. It will create a culture of love— an atmosphere permeated by the Fruit of the Spirit, that is, the presence of Jesus.

A Community of Loving Oneness

Then, comes the clincher in Jesus' third request: "May they also be [one] in us *so that* the world may believe that you have sent me." John 17:21

Jesus mentions this "cause and effect" twice in His prayer: the world will know Jesus is real when His church loves like Jesus. In other words, the **credibility of our evangelist message will be in direct proportion to how successfully we are in allowing the Spirit of God to flow through us in creating a loving community of oneness.**

So Jesus prayed that we would be:
1. *Sanctified:* Recognize that we are set apart for the filling of His Fruit of His Holy Spirit which will transform our characters to be like the love of Jesus.
2. *Changed:* So we may become one community of love, joy, peace, patience, kindness, goodness, faithfulness, gentleness and self-control.
3. *Impacted*: So that because of this loving community the world will see the difference in our characters and recognize that only a holy God could bring such a change. Then they will be attracted to our message and to our God.

The credibility of your church pivots upon how fully the Fruit of the Spirit has been allowed to recreate your congregation into a community of love, joy, peace, patience, kindness, goodness, faithfulness, gentleness, and self-control. You'll know this is happening when neighbors start referring to your members as "those people who love so well." By seeing, they, too, might believe.

Don't you wish Gandhi could have said: "I like you Christians because you are so loving, just like your Christ"?

Let me say something more about this "community of loving oneness" which was at the core of His dying prayer.

There are many types of groups: fraternities, secret societies, clubs, teams, political organizations, and churches. But what will cause your community members to turn their heads with amazement because of your church? Will it be because of what your church preaches against? Will it be the awesome structure or campus you have built? Will it be your great choir or awesome Christmas program?

NO! According to Jesus, *what will turn the unbeliever's head and cause him/her to be attracted to your church is the inclusive, nonjudgmental, never-let-you-go kind of love that makes you and your church community beautifully unique.*

The Acid Test for Your Church

And now the tough part. It's easy for a church to be a "friendly" church or call itself the "loving" church. In fact while traveling on a Rhode Island back road, I found an old wood-framed church with its name proudly displayed: "The Amicable Church."

It's easy to love when things are going well. The real test that will be the witness to the community of the power of your church will be how you handle conflict. And, unfortunately, churches are renowned for handling conflict VERY badly. Congregations split. Churches call each other names and condemn. They gossip. They manipulate. They practice selfishness under the cloak of "God is blessing us with prosperity."

To the unbeliever, this hypocrisy is unbelievably apparent. Pollster George Barna confirms our fears when he says that surveys show that church members are not noticeably different than unbelievers in their moral behavior.

SO, what will turn the unbeliever's head and plant a desire in them to know what you believe? "By this everyone will know that you are my disciples, if you love one another." John 13:35

When you extend forgiveness instead of slander or revenge... they will notice.

When you sacrifice and go without so that someone in need is loved, fed, or clothed... they will notice.

When you love and care rather than isolate and criticize... they will notice.

When you're willing to step out of the spotlight so that someone else can be applauded... they will notice.

When you are willing to lose a contract because you refuse to cheat or lie... they will notice.

When you can put your arm around someone of a different faith or different political persuasion or opposing views on homosexuality or abortion and say,, "I disagree with you but love you anyway"... the world will take note that there is something very, very, VERY different and very healthy about you.

THAT is the result of the visible presence of the Holy Spirit transforming in you the character of Jesus.
THEN the world will know that Jesus came and is real AND can really change people's dark, selfish heart.
As I compare these three concerns in Jesus' prayer to the church of my youth, I see that my church had an incomplete understanding of why they existed:
1. Instead of "sanctified" (meaning "being filled and transformed by God's Spirit to reflect Jesus' love) the message I heard was: "Be perfect as measured by our list of correct behavior."
2. Instead of Jesus' plea that the church become a "community of loving oneness," I heard that we should be a community of love—through conformity, where all

would believe and act similar least one be ostracized as being deceived or worldly.
3. Instead of understanding that how we love each other that would give our witness its greatest credibility, I heard that we should agitate, confront, even irritate so that people might listen to our concept of "the truth," because to believe differently meant that they would be eternally lost.

Because this most important second step was mostly ignored or just given lip service (and the third step misunderstood) the negative result was too often a spirit of judgmentalism, that is, one's spirituality measured by the evil he avoided and religious things she did.

Does that define your church as well?

It seemed that the greatest fear was, "What will others within the church think?" We wanted to appear holy, hide our imperfections, and pretend to be doing better than we really were, all the while feeling guilty knowing we weren't doing enough. Others who weren't as "spiritual" needed to shape up or ship out because they were like Achans in the camp[41] — blocking God's blessing for the rest of us!

It was not a "safe" place to grow. And there were a few Mrs. Smiths who felt called by God to point out the imperfections of others. "I must call sin by its right name" seemed to be their motto, with little hesitation in confronting a member or guest with their pious corrective judgments.

This prayer of Jesus is now the bedrock, driving passion of my ministry. I want to foster churches that are so positive, so

---

[41] In Joshua 7 the camp of Israel experienced many bad things because Achan had committed a terrible sin against the Lord. They all suffered because of his sin, kind of like the whole 3rd grade class not being allowed to go out to recess until the guilty person confessed to letting loose the snake in the classroom.

contagious, that God feels it is safe to direct broken people to them for healing.

I can hear it now. "Oh pastor, I think the church is losing its way and everybody is talking about love, love, love. Shouldn't we get back to focusing again on right doctrine, proper dress and obedience because these are troubling times?"

Remember, Jesus is searching not just for a loving wife, but for a loyal one as well. Loyal means faithfulness and obedience. But obedience based on duty is idolatry, while obedience that flows from a heart filled with God's Spirit is one of love, joy, peace, unpretentious, and nonjudgmental.

Right Doctrine Is Measured By What It Produces

If your church doctrines and how they are applied don't create a culture of nonjudgmental love, joy, and peace based upon knowing and loving Jesus, then either the doctrine is wrong or the application is wrong. Jesus is clear about the acid test for the church: "By this everyone will know that you are my disciples, if you love one another." John 13:35

Listen, if the straight-laced church of yesterday were the answer to Jesus' prayer in His effort to find both a loyal and loving spiritual wife, then He would have come and taken her home to the great heavenly wedding feast promised when He said, "I go to prepare a place for you... and I will come again to take to home to be with me." John 14:1-3 (NKJV)

But He didn't take her home because she wasn't and isn't both the loyal and loving wife He is searching for. God would not have enjoyed living with her forever any more than he enjoyed living with the Pharisaical church of Jesus' day. Above everything else, **He's looking for a loyal and loving wife that He can ENJOY forever.**

Do you see why I believe that heaven is not merely for people who at some time "accepted Jesus" but is for disciples who will ENJOY living with Jesus—since in the here and now they embrace God's Spirit in a transforming manner. Simply put, their characters are like Jesus. Heaven is for those who in their hearts are "married" to Jesus, who love Him and want to live in His presence forever.

Doesn't this make a truck load of sense? If you are being sanctified and filled with the Holy Spirit, it will manifest itself in the Fruit of the Spirit. And the Fruit of the Spirit really is a definition of the character of Jesus. So when you talk about having Jesus in your heart you should be talking about His Spirit growing in you His love, His joy, and His peaceable character. We're talking about a wife who is nurturing a "what-EVER it takes to please and glorify you, Lord" attitude.

Wow, what a wife! And THAT makes her (the church) very attractive not only to Jesus but to the unbeliever as well.

Think about this. Why would an unbeliever want to come to your church? Jesus prayed that the primary attraction will be that they see people of diverse backgrounds and temperaments AND differing convictions on some Bible doctrines coming together in loving oneness. Not in conformity, but loving unity. There is such an obvious pervasive spirit of love, joy, peace, kindness amongst your congregation that they go, "Wow! How does that happen? Maybe I should check this out and see what they have that I don't, because I haven't seen that kind of spirit among any other people. That looks like a safe place to grow and to explore my questions about God."

Heaven is for lovers—people who long for an eternity of loving Jesus and being loved in return. Someday all that gets in the way of this loving relationship (the pain, loneliness, the separation, the silence) will be done away.

John the Revelator writes: "I heard a loud voice from the throne saying, 'Look! God's dwelling place is now among the people, and he will dwell with them. They will be his people, and God himself will be with them and be their God. He will wipe every tear from their eyes. There will be no more death or mourning or crying or pain, for the old order of things has passed away.'" Revelation 21:3-4

Long-distance engagements are not easy. I graduated from a college near the Napa valley in California and then packed up and drove over 2200 miles to my seminary in Michigan. I lived in a bachelor dormitory where my room was 6' x 10" (NO lie!). Five of us guys lived in a block of these cubicles and shared a small common kitchen and sitting area. You have no idea what a small under-the-counter refrigerator can smell like until you room with a Lebanese, a southern Black, an Australian, and a California intellectual.

I was going steady with a girl back home and every day I sealed and mailed my love letter. By Thanksgiving I knew that one year of these bachelors and the distance from my lover was enough. I had it all planned out: where we would be when I proposed and what I might say. I couldn't wait.

So at the beginning of my Thanksgiving break I boarded the plan at Chicago's O'Hare International airport and settled in for the long flight. Why is it that when you're very anxious to get somewhere that it seems to take twice as long. FINALLY, I felt the plane dip and start its descent into San Francisco International.

The jet-way was connected and the door opened. Everyone who flies knows how frustratingly slow everyone is in disembarking. Crouched in a semi-standing position at my seat I had an impulsive urge to just crawl across all the seats and get off that plane.

Finally, I was out... striding up the jet-way and into the terminal. Standing in a row of smiles was my brother, his wife, my mom, and dad. It was great to see them but I was looking for something more... someone other.

And then I spotted her behind the rest. The pink dress with the frills (that she had made for herself), the perfume, the hair that must have taken hours (how long DID it take her to get ready?). And then the warm blue eyes, dimples and seductive smile! THAT was whom I was most waiting to see. We were finally together.

In a few days I did "the ask" and her answer was accompanied with a smile and very tight, long hug. My bride and I would be together "until death do us part." And... we are still together. Over forty-seven years and we're already talking about what we want to do to celebrate our fiftieth.

Heaven Is for Lovers

Heaven is when Jesus (the groom) and His bride (us) are finally together... to love, to laugh, to share, to learn, to explore. But there will not be an "until death do us part" because death will be a thing of the past. Heaven will be forever.

Several years ago my wife and I had the privilege of seeing the Matterhorn in Zermatt, Switzerland (one of our favorite "together" things is to travel). It's breathtaking. And we learned something quite interesting. The weather on the mountain is unpredictable. You can begin your climb in bright sun and clear skies, but in a very short time it can become covered with clouds.

We learned that a very interesting phenomenon has been noted about amateur climbers. If they can see the summit, they climb with energy and a quicker pace. But when the summit is obscured by clouds, when they cannot see their objective, they tire more quickly, grumble, complain, and often give up.

Church members who have an unclear or incorrect idea of what the church should be, or members who have lost sight of that objective, tend to become weary, distracted, complaining, argumentative, and judgmental. But in Jesus' dying prayer, He pled with the Father that you would never lose sight of His dream for you, that you would become a congregation of such powerful whatEVER nonjudgmental love that people just won't be able to stay away. Whatever it is that you have, they desperately want.

I pray that you will become the whatEVER disciple, wife, and church that will be the answer to Jesus' prayer and one that He would enjoy living with forever. I know that Jesus is definitely looking forward to that day when our transport through space brings us to our new home that He has prepared. There we will meet him face to face . . . in a heavenly embrace.

Imagination Station #14

I pray these "Imagination Stations" have infused a small dose of "What if?" and "Wow!" serum into your thoughts about heaven?

To add to your enjoyment, I have created a one-hour multimedia presentation, featuring some these imaginative ideas into sound and picture. With special effect glasses and creative stage lighting, against a backdrop of imaginative videos and awesomely beautiful music, you and others will experience an imaginary journey into what heaven might be.

For a minimal fee, a presentation at your church can be made available. My greatest reward is seeing the excitement in viewers' eyes and hearing the anticipation in their voice. Never will I forget one little elderly lady shuffling out the door after such a presentation and looking up at me with a sparkle in her weary eyes. "I can't wait to ski in heaven," she said, with a wink.

To view a five-minute sampler of what you can experience in this live multimedia presentation "Snowboarding in Heaven," please copy and paste this online address into your computer: https://vimeo.com/159863796.

To host this presentation at your facility, please contact: Dr. Terry Pooler, 518 Zachary Dr, Apopka, Fl, 32712; tgpooler46@gmail.com.